Toy Stories

Photos of Children from Around the World and Their Favorite Things

Gabriele Galimberti

Introduction by Ben Machell

Abrams Image
New York

An introduction

by Ben Machell

If someone asked you to describe your favorite childhood toys, the chances are you would not have to think too hard about it. So many early memories become hazy and indistinct over time, but precise details of the toys we loved somehow endure: the specific smell of a stuffed bunny rabbit; the thrill of gripping the hilt of a plastic sword; the sound and feel of your small hand rummaging through a large box of LEGO bricks. Toys are the first things over which we feel any real ownership, and as children, we cared about them more ferociously than we would probably like to admit now.

On one level, this is why Gabriele Galimberti's work is so affecting. Few subjects could be more inclusive than toys and childhood. All that the viewer requires to appreciate these photographs are empathy and memory. "In some ways, it is a very simple project," Galimberti explains. "You don't necessarily need to know all about the history of photography, or have an in-depth understanding of different photographic techniques, in order to appreciate the images. My eighty-five-year-old grandmother doesn't know where some of the countries I visited are—places like Zambia, Malawi, or Fiji—but she remembers her favorite toys. Everybody does."

Galimberti's journey around the world photographing children and their toys lasted thirty months and took him to fifty-eight countries. The project began, however, just a few miles from his home in Castiglion Fiorentino, Tuscany. Commissioned to provide a portrait of a "typical Tuscan child," he drove to a nearby farm to photograph four-year-old Alessia, who had been playing with an array of colorful plastic farming implements. "I decided to lay out the toys on the ground in front of her," says Galimberti. "Immediately, there was something about the composition I liked."

As work took him around the world—from Alaska to Haiti, Fiji, Australia, Southeast Asia, India, Europe, Africa, and, finally, South America—Galimberti repeated this composition over and over. "For every photograph, I would spend the entire day with the family. In some places, like China and the Middle East, the parents would push their children hard to pose for the photos, even if the kids didn't seem comfortable. It could be a bit embarrassing. I didn't want to take pictures of crying children." Elsewhere, in places like South America, the parents seemed relaxed to the point of ambivalence. "They said I could do whatever I wanted, provided their children didn't mind."

Time and again, Galimberti was struck by how the toys presented to him revealed something about the economic and social reality in which the children lived. While young Tuscan farm girl Alessia played with plastic farm tools, one child from an affluent family in a booming Chinese city loved playing Monopoly. Four-year-old Abel Sientes Armas from Nopaltepec, Mexico, lived near a major sugar cane plantation, and grew up seeing endless convoys of big trucks rumbling down his road. His favorite toys? "Big" trucks, arranged for Galimberti in an endless circular convoy.

These toys, Galimberti began to realize, said as much about the mothers and fathers as they did about the children themselves. "I learned more about being a parent than I did about being a child from this whole process," he says. Hopes and ambitions are passed down through the toys parents choose for their children. Children from families boasting musicians invariably receive toy instruments. Ralf, from Riga in Latvia, had countless toy cars bestowed on him by his taxi-driver mother, who named him after racing driver Ralf Schumacher. She loves cars. Now he does, too.

However, this dynamic only applied in countries where parents could pick and choose which toys their children could have. In areas of poverty, the difference was striking. "I ended up in a small village in northern Zambia where there was nothing. No electricity, no water, and, of course, no toy shops. But the children had found a box of sunglasses—I think it fell off a truck—and the glasses became their favorite toys. Actually, their only toys. They would play 'market,' buying and selling the glasses to each other, sharing everything between them."

Again, this reflected a broader pattern. The fewer toys a child had, the less possessive he or she was about them. Galimberti describes having to spend several hours winning the trust of Western children before they would consent to let him touch their planes, cars, or dolls. "In poorer countries, they don't care as much. They play in a different way, running around, sharing one ball between them all."

Likewise, children who enjoy a free-roaming existence in the countryside seemed to place less value on their toys than children living in busy cities, confined and isolated. "City children mostly stay inside, and mostly play alone," he says. "They tend to have a lot more toys and to be a lot more possessive."

Still, there were occasions when touching coincidences would exist between children living thousands of miles apart. In the United States, a boy named Orly loved plastic dinosaurs. In Malawi, a boy named Chiwa loved a plastic dinosaur too, a green triceratops given to him by an NGO worker. They both maintained that their dinosaurs protected them at night—in Orly's case, from the threat of "kidnappers"; in Chiwa's case, from dangerous animals and venomous insects.

Galimberti says that, more than anything, this project was fun—a simple and heartfelt conclusion to a simple and heartfelt project. And though that's not to say there aren't poignancy and truth within these images, the fact remains that stepping into a young child's world and playing with his or her toys will always be a gentle pleasure.

Ben Machell is a feature writer for *The Times* of London. He was also a fully paid-up member of the LEGO Club as a kid.

Orly, 4

Brownsville, Texas

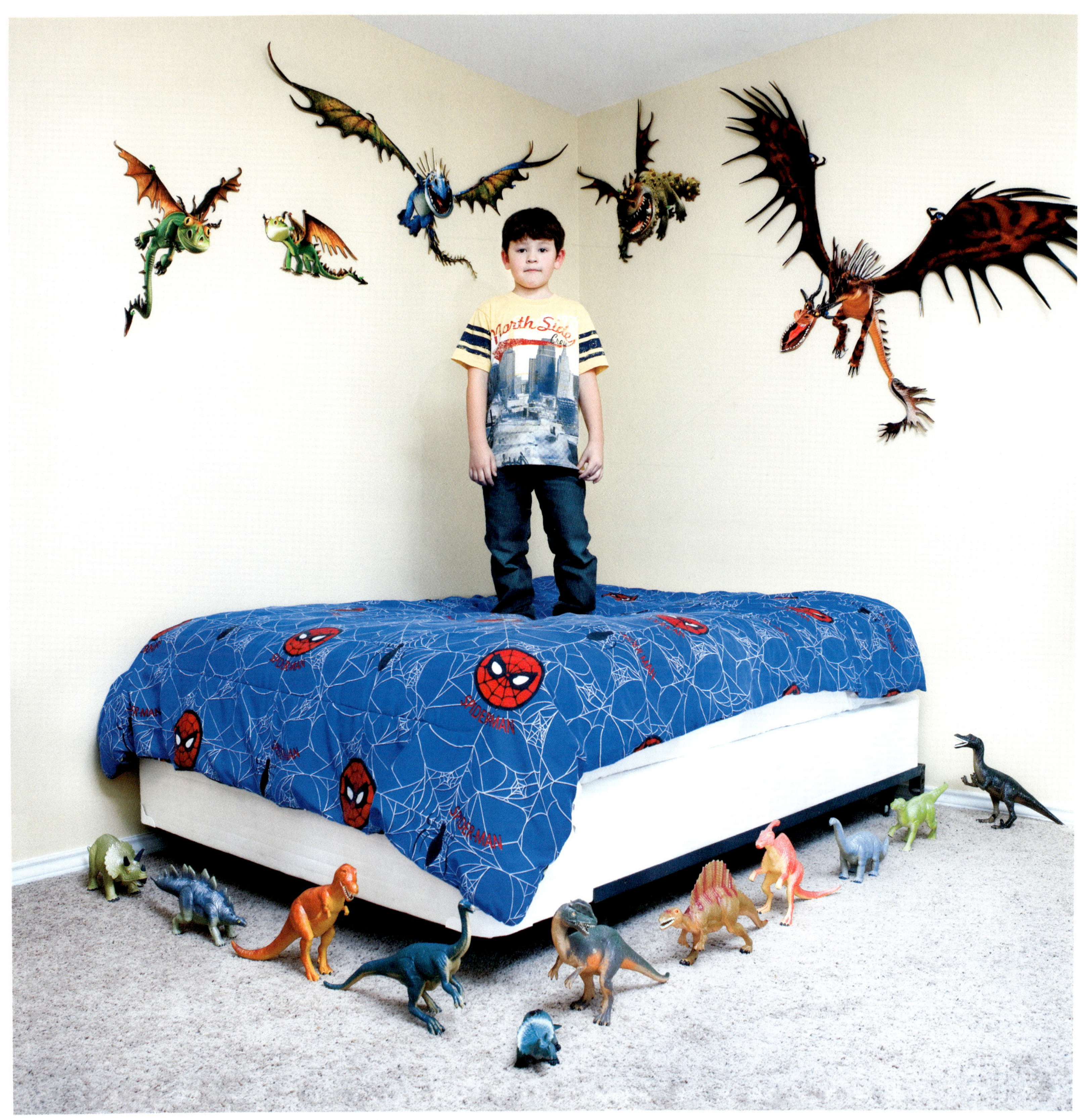
North Side
SPIDER-MAN

Bethsaida, 4

Port-au-Prince, Haiti

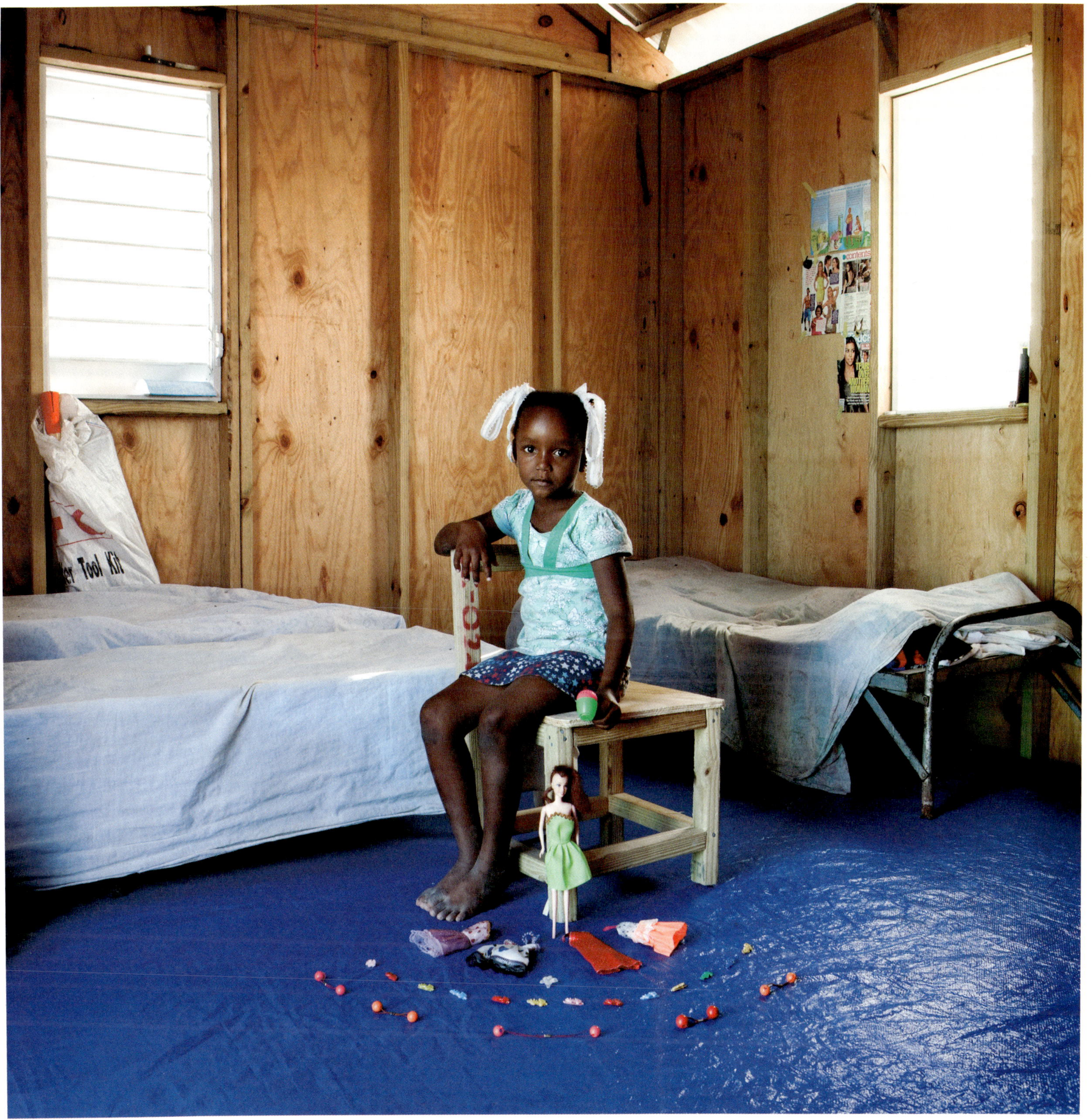
Tool Kit

Mikkel, 3

Bergen, Norway

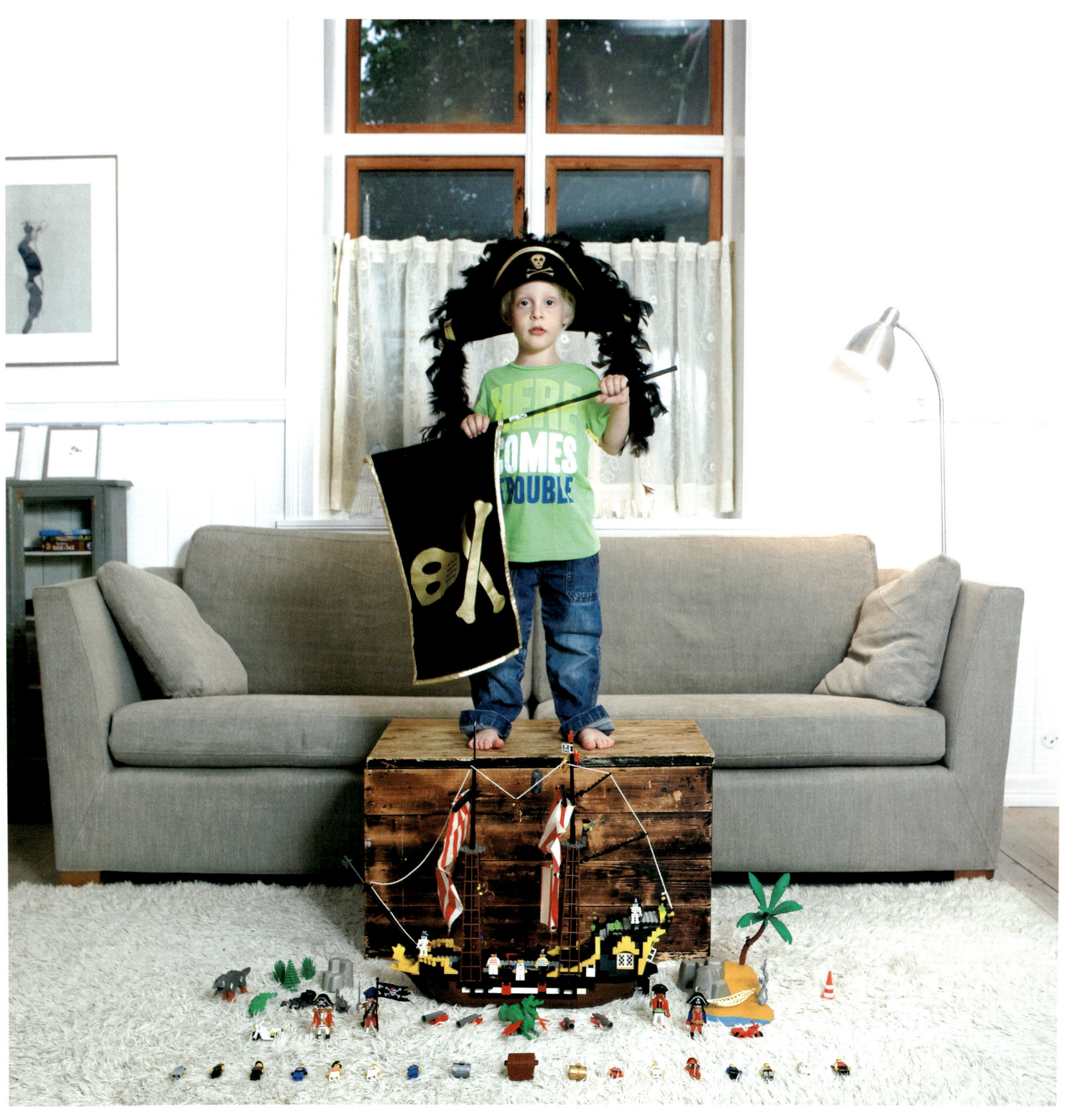

Allenah, 4

El Nido, Philippines

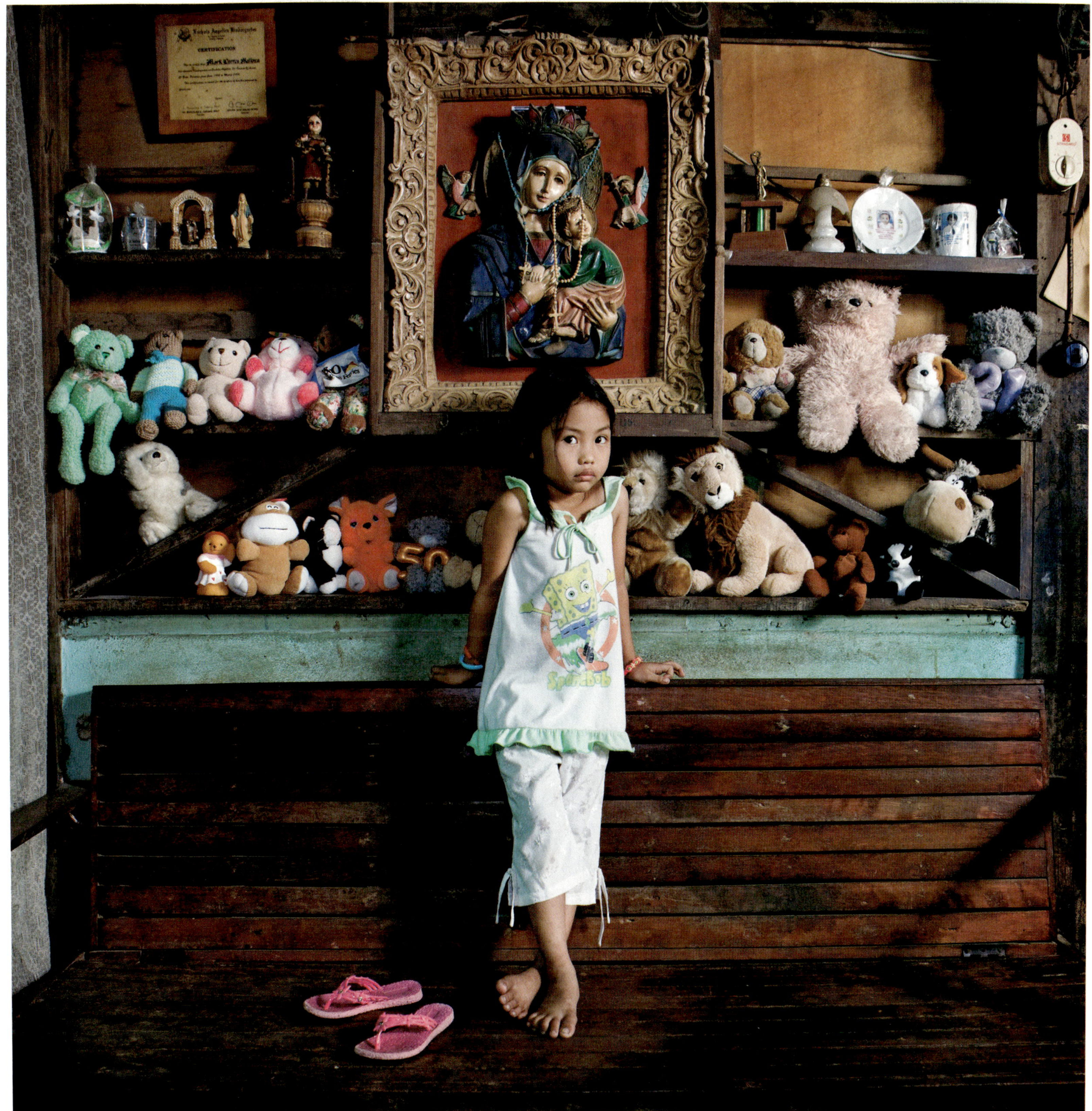

Taha, 4

Beirut, Lebanon

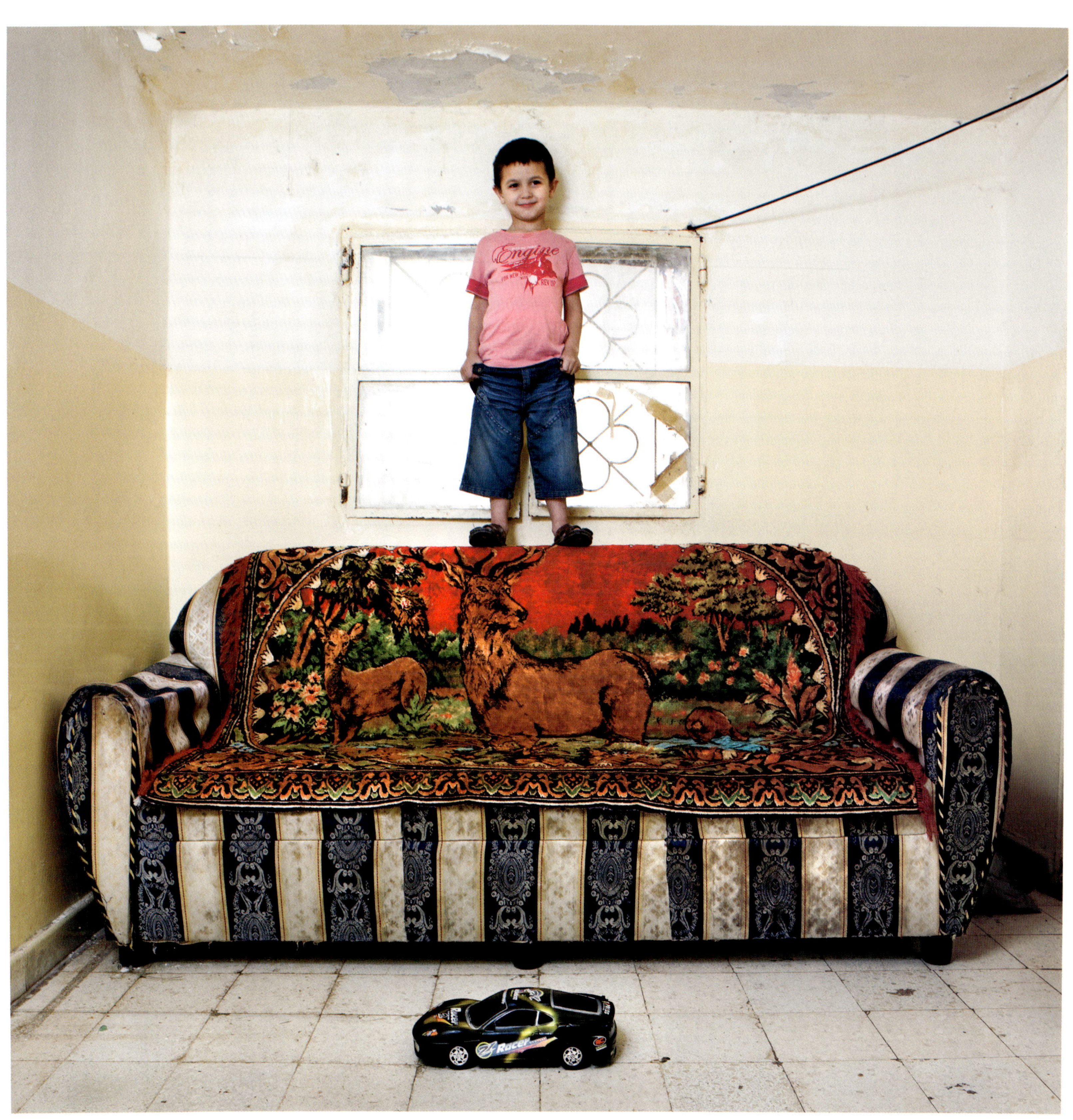
Engine
Racer

Julia, 3

Tirana, Albania

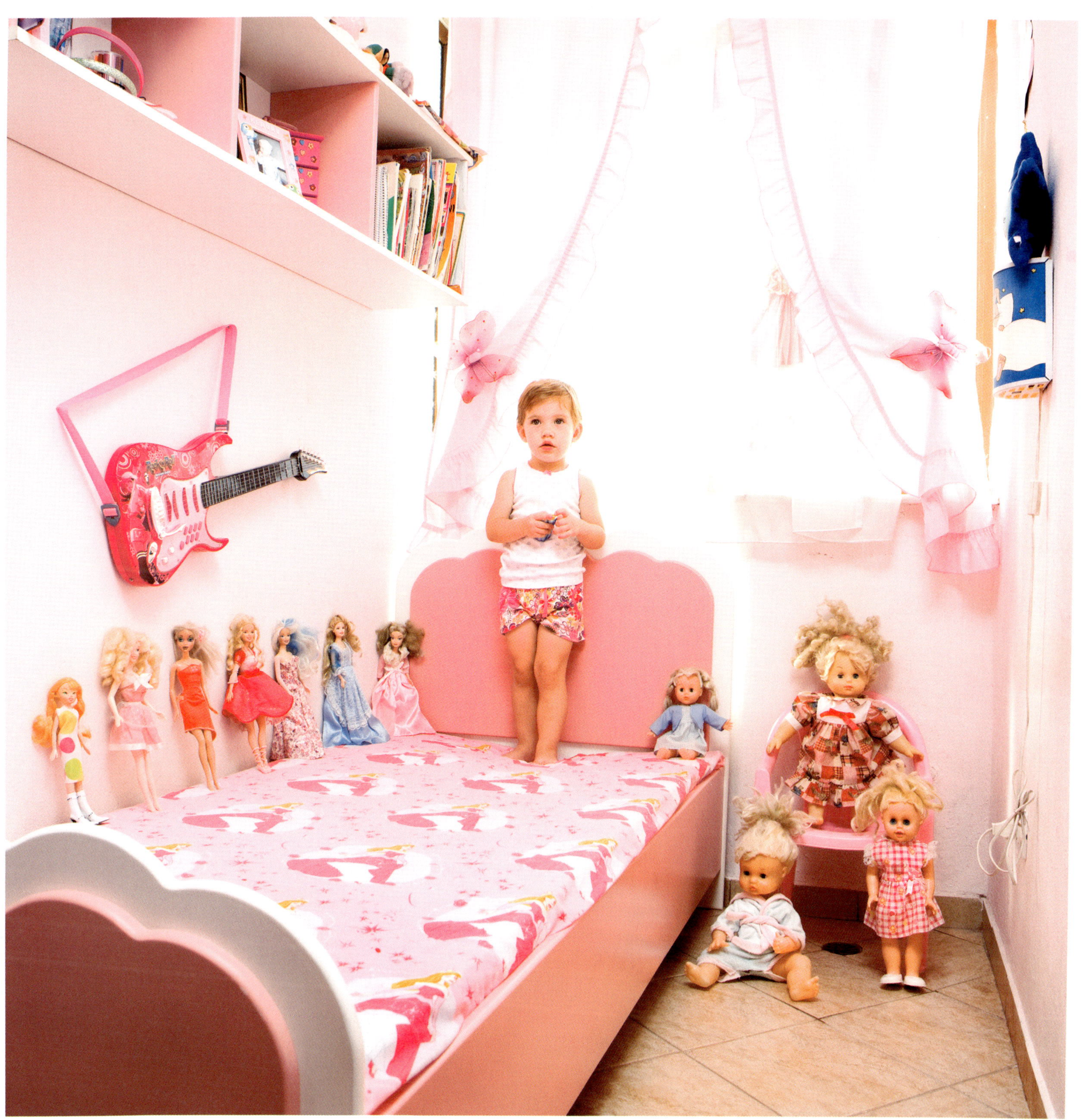

Tangawizi, 3

Keekorok, Kenya

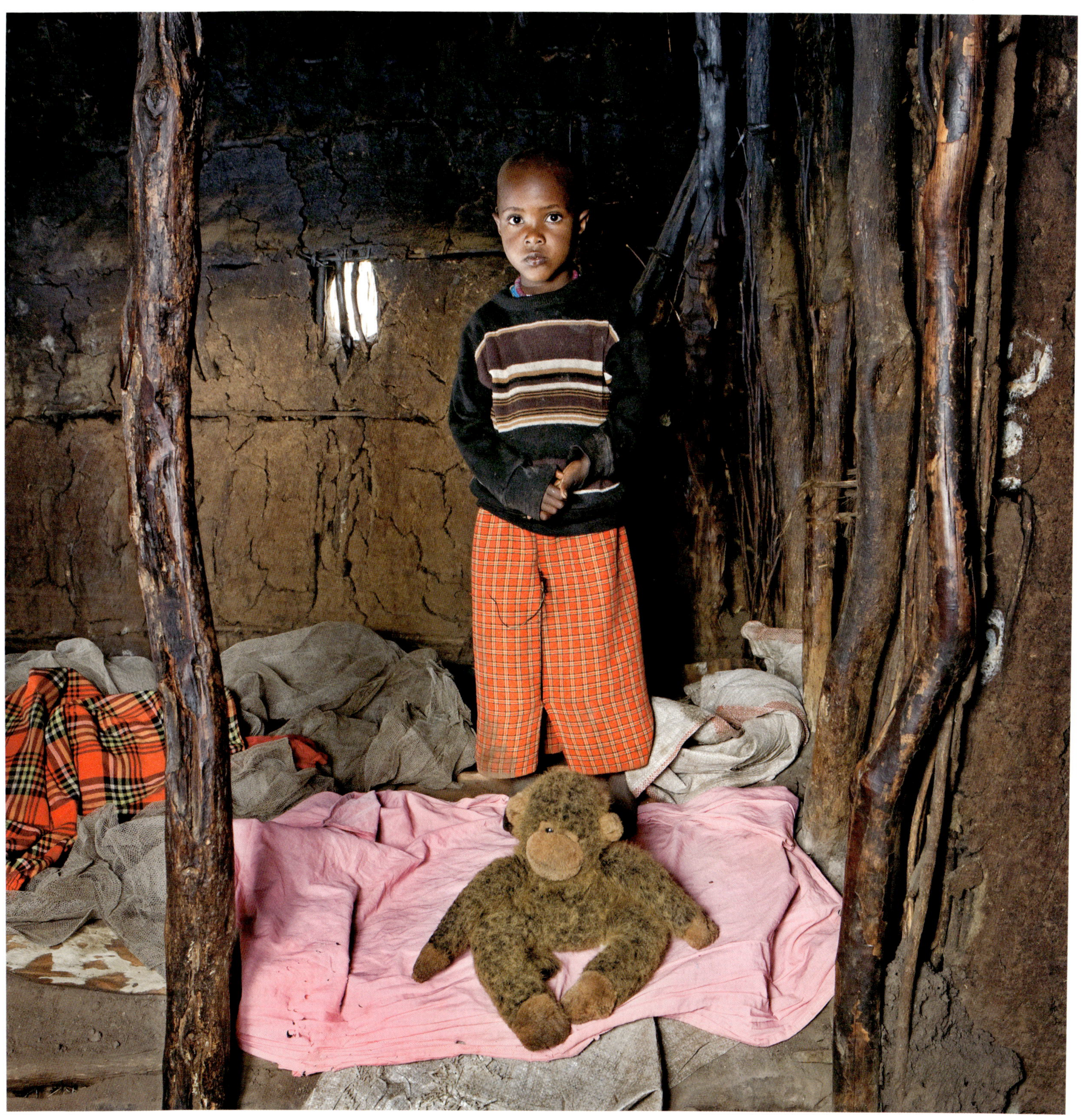

Cun Zi Yi, 3

Chongqing, China

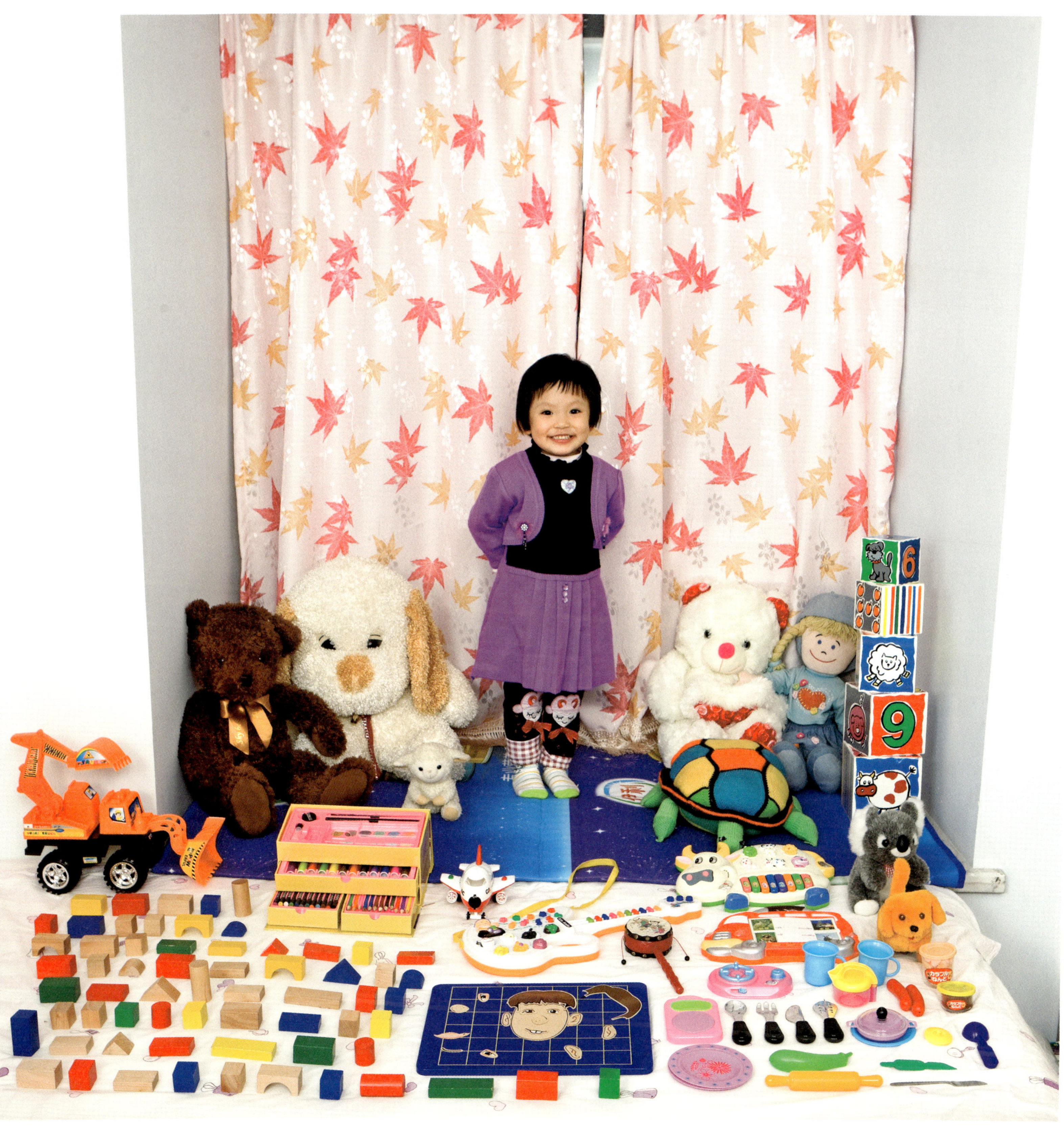
6
9

Julius, 3

Lausanne, Switzerland

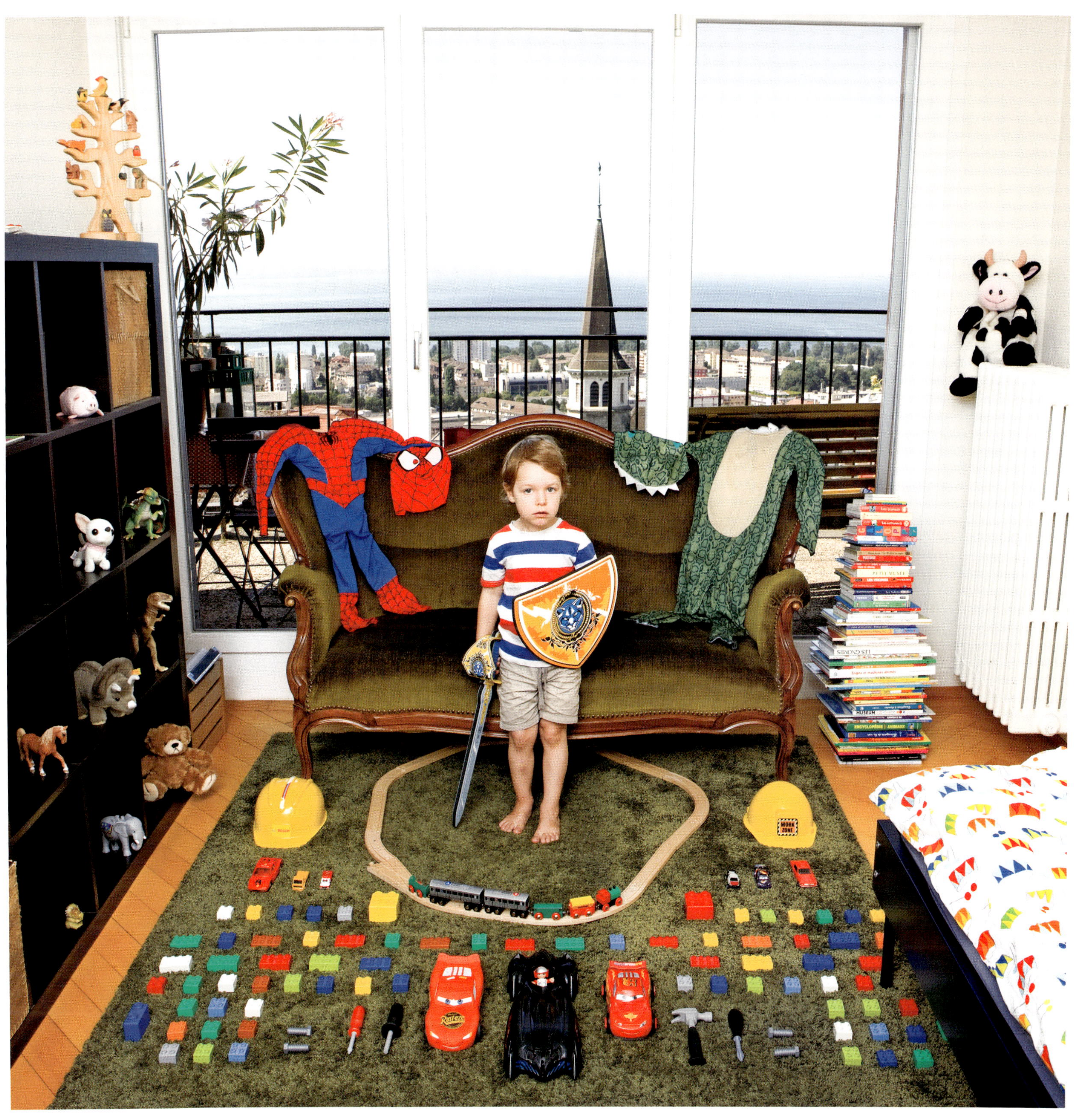
Les oiseaux
PETIT MUSÉE
LES VIKINGS
LES GNOMES
Engins et machines animés
MUSEUM
ENCYCLOPÉDIE ANIMAUX
WORK ZONE

Arafa & Aisha, 5

Bububu, Zanzibar

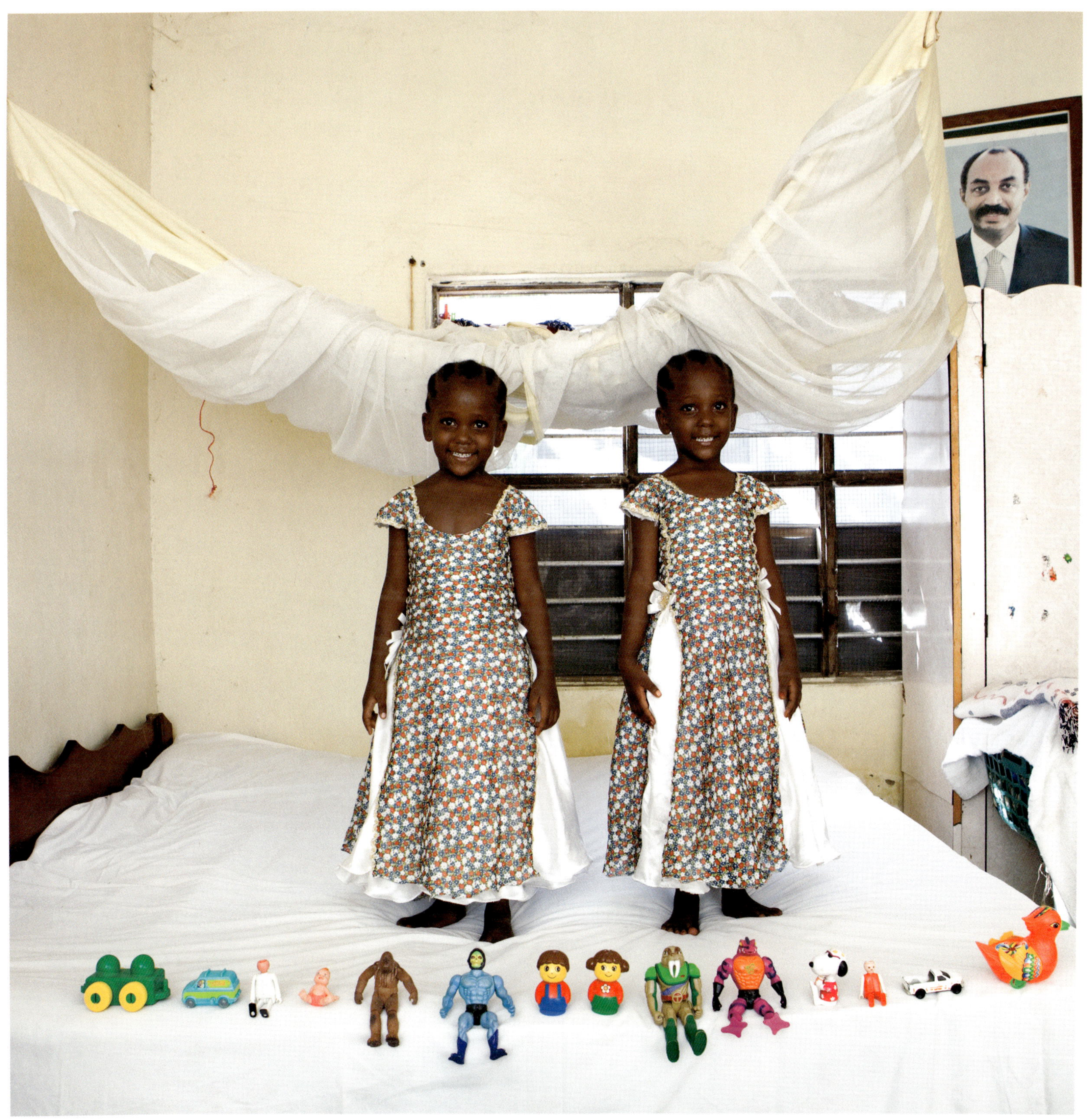

Lucas, 3

Sydney, Australia

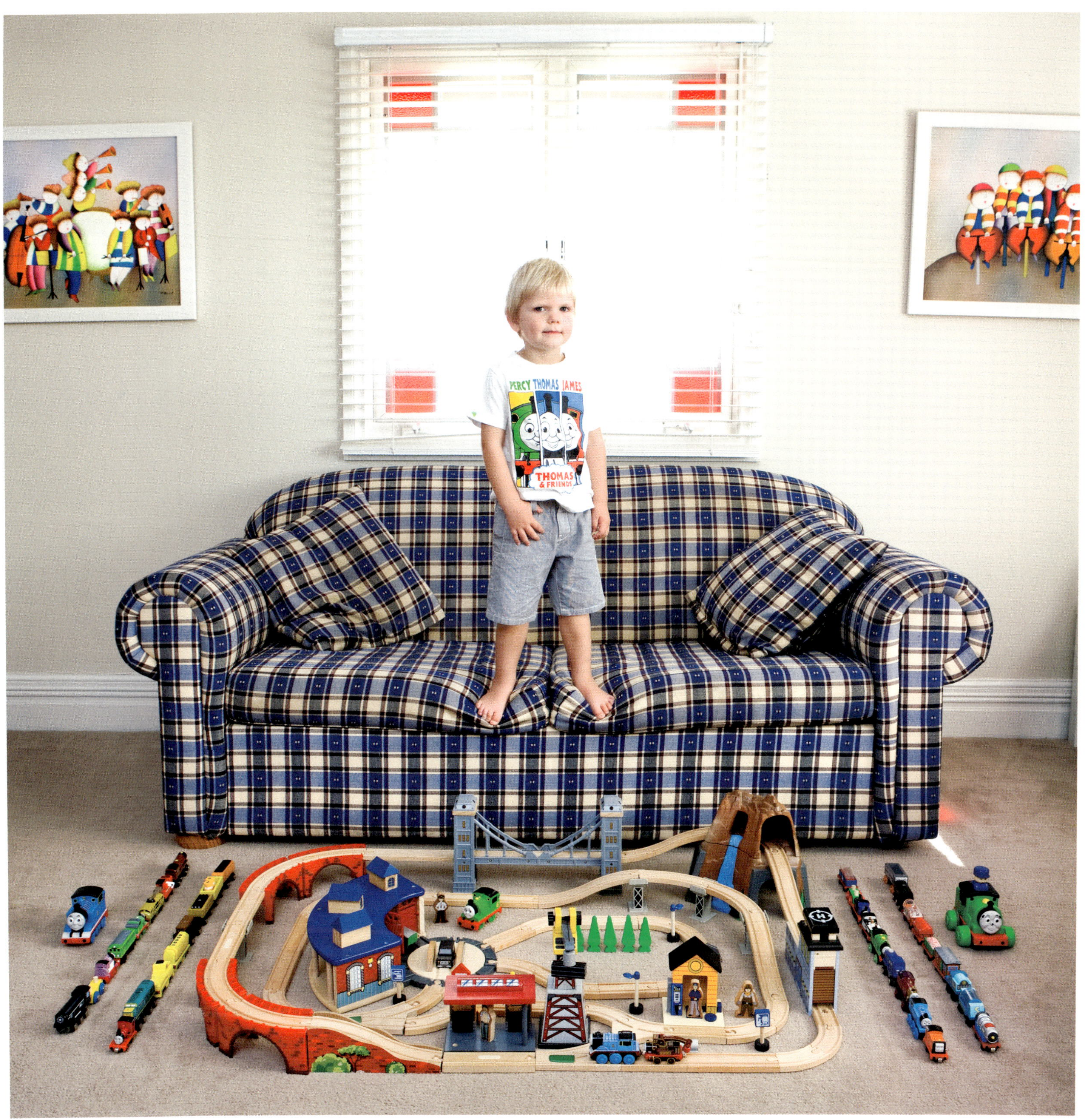
PERCY THOMAS JAMES
THOMAS
& FRIENDS

Reania, 3

Kuala Lumpur, Malaysia

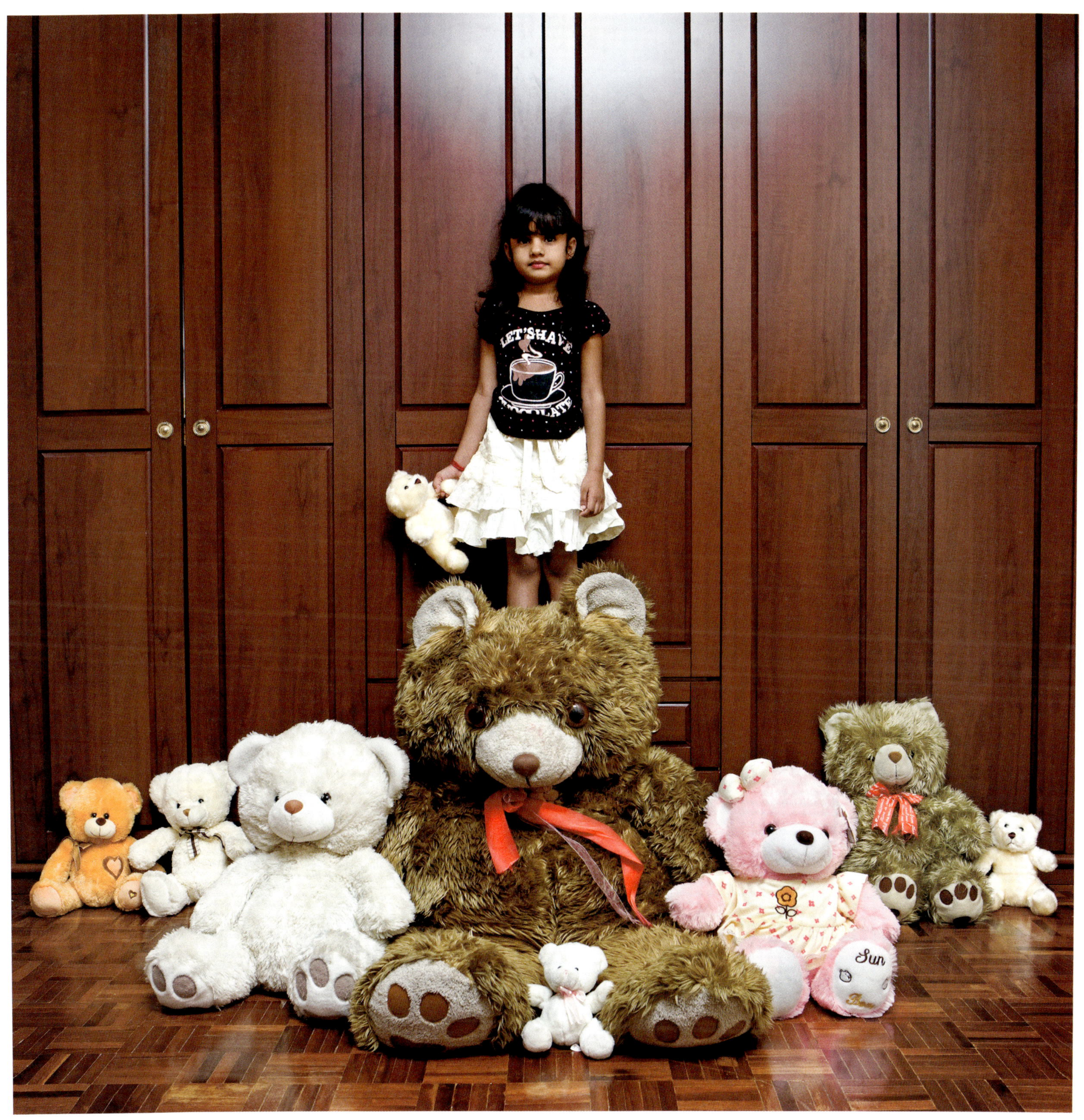
LET'S HAVE
Sun

Callum, 4

Fairbanks, Alaska

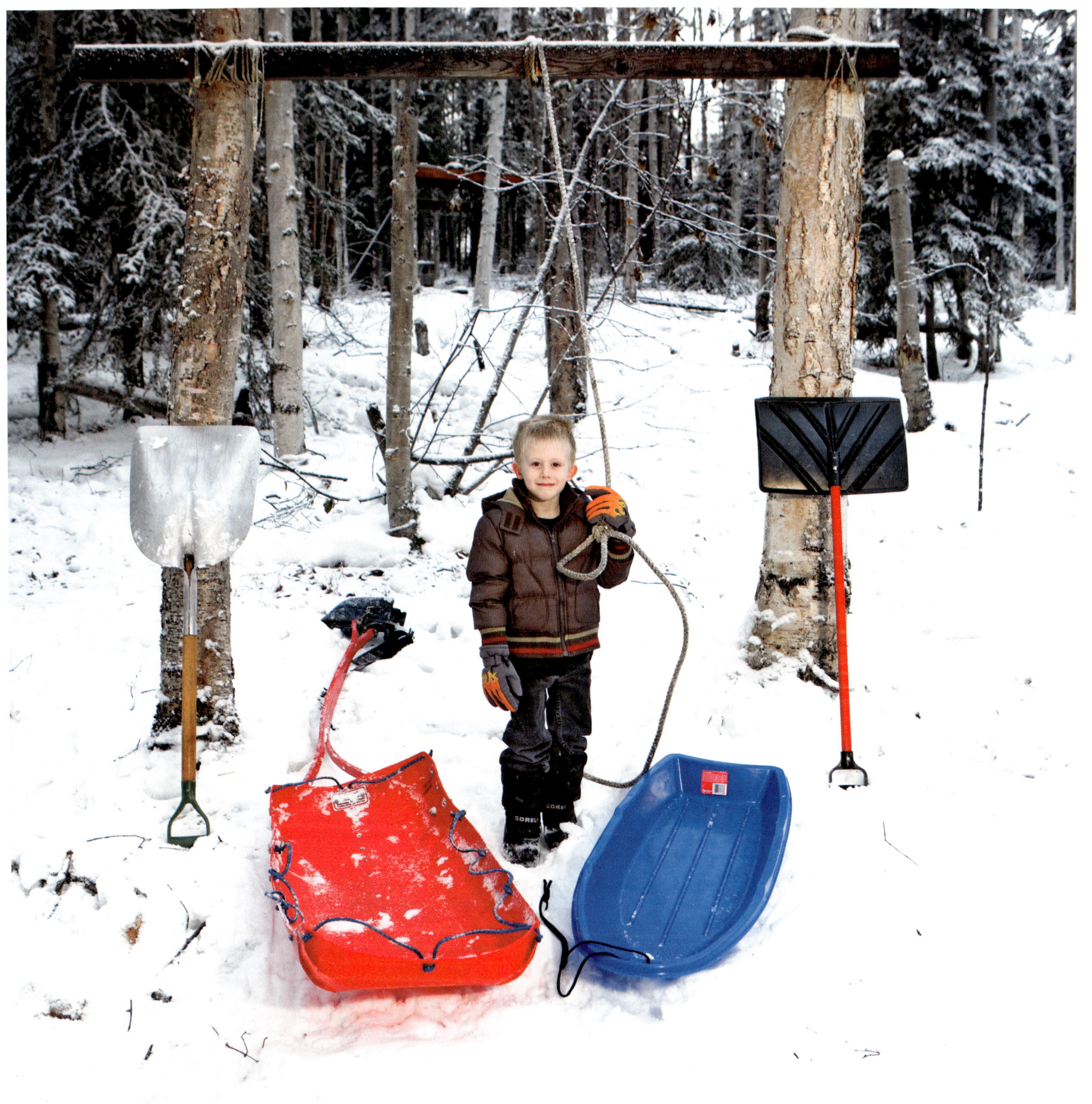
SOREL
SOREL

Tyra, 3

Stockholm, Sweden

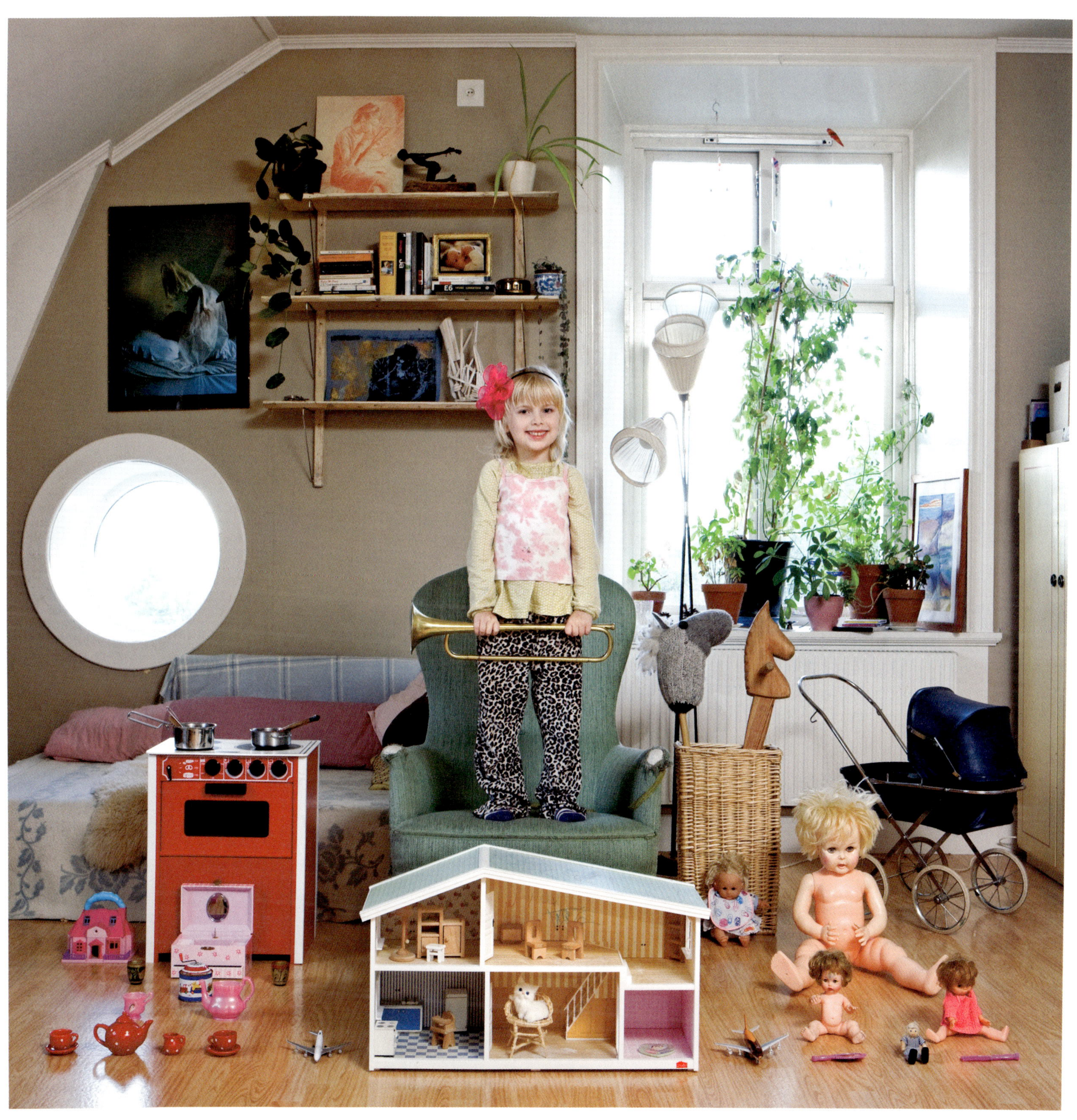

Li Yi, 5

Shenyang, China

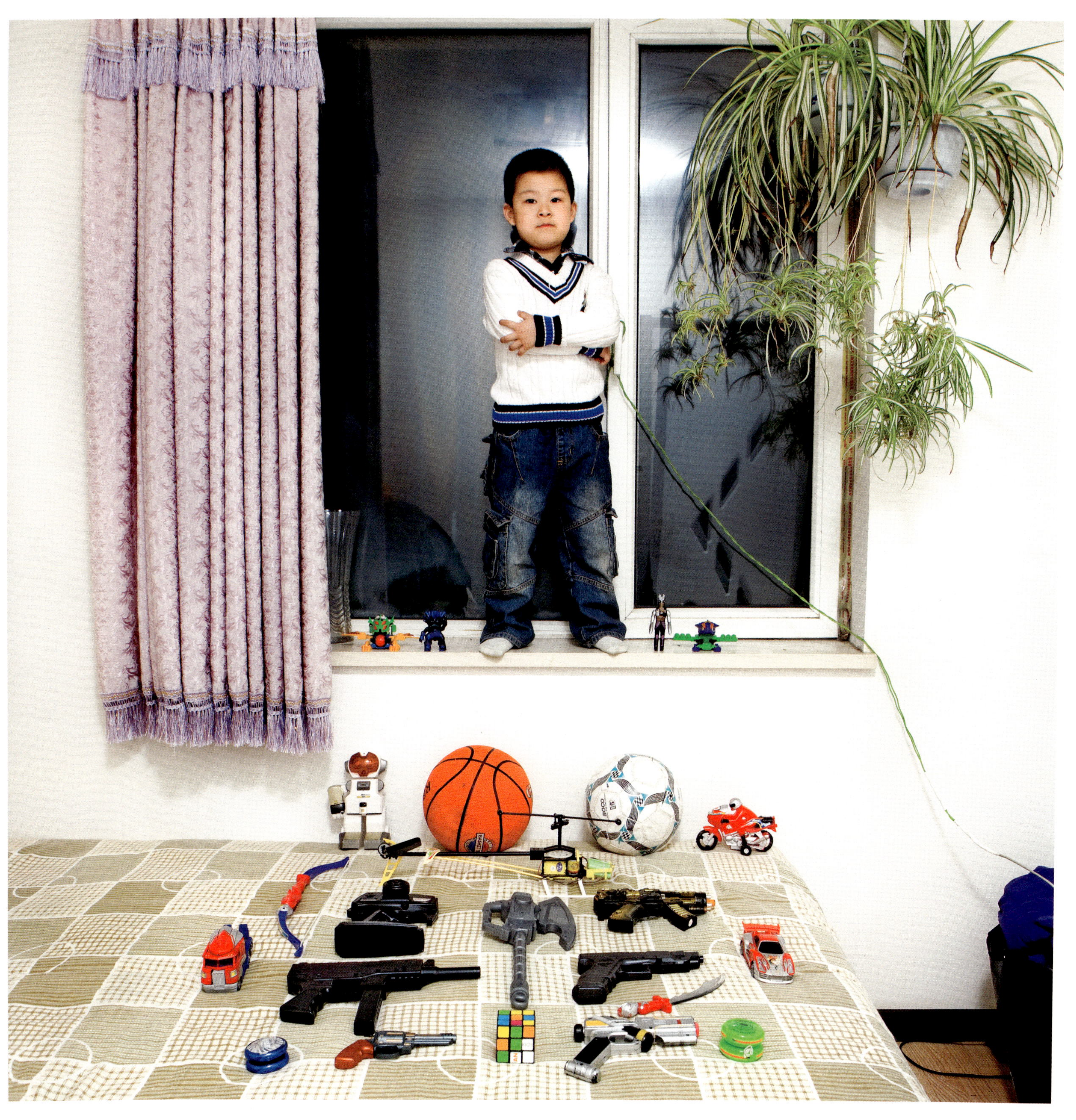

Maudy, 3

Kalulushi, Zambia

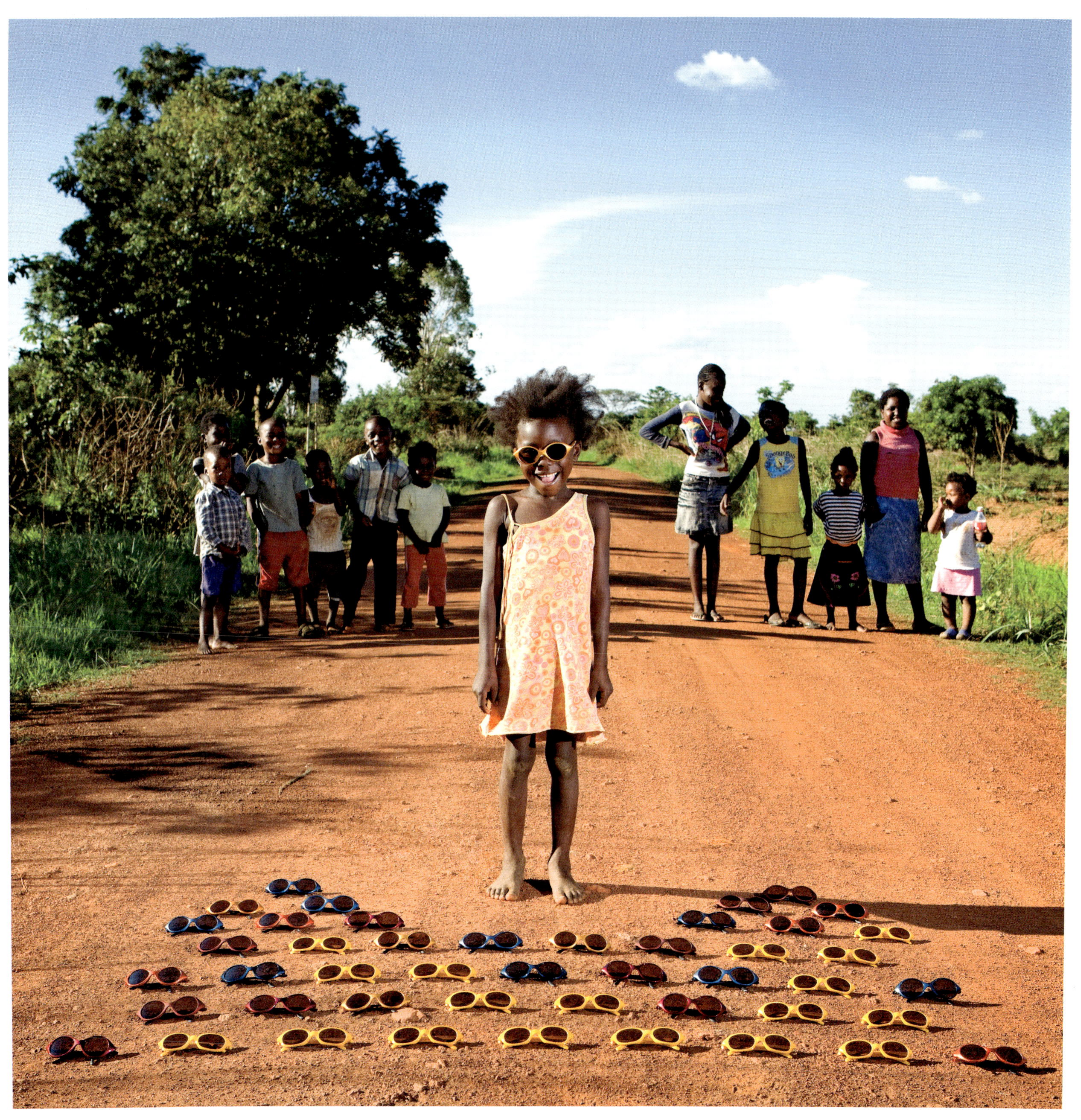

Henry, 5

Berkeley, California

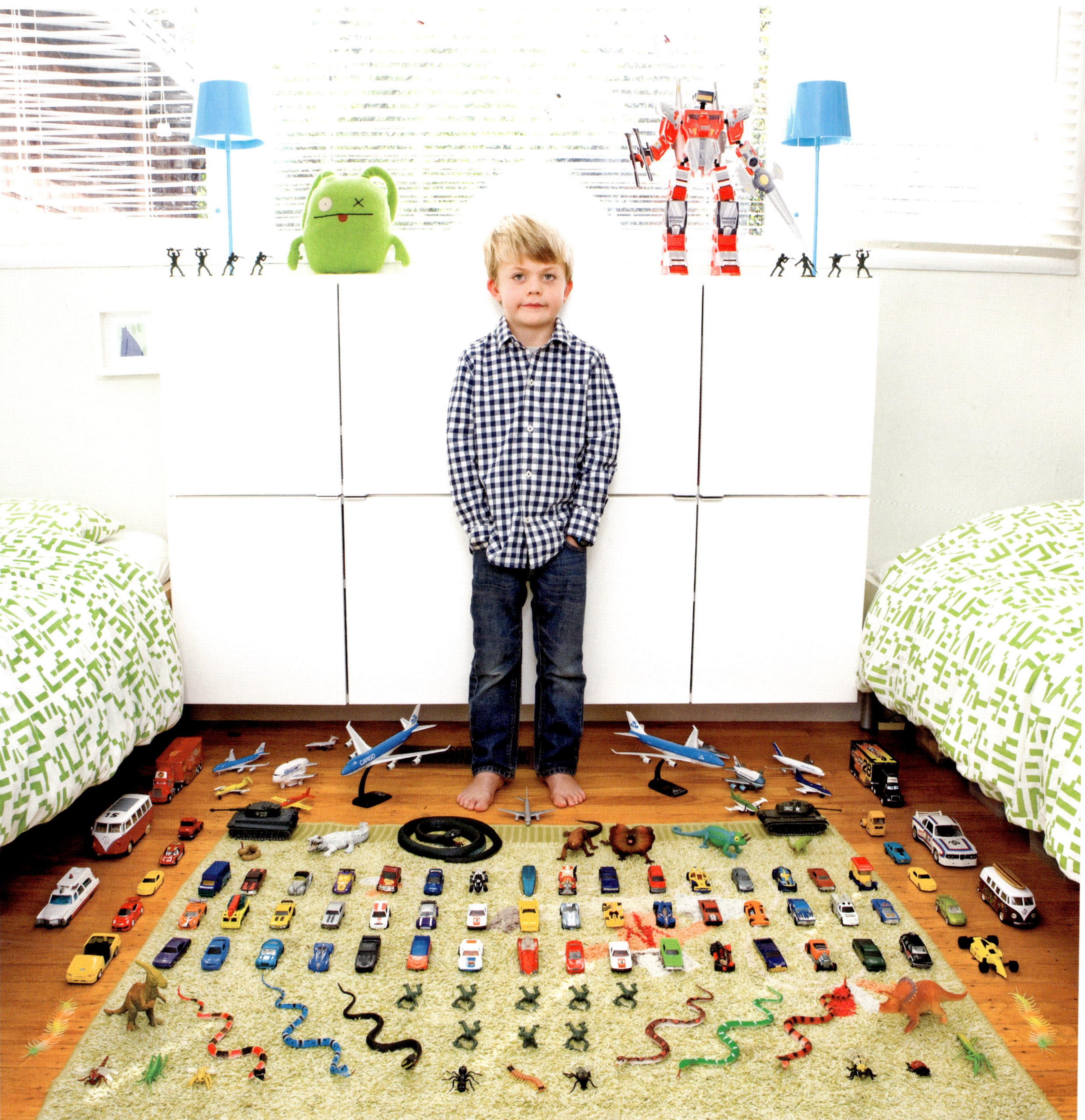

Talia, 5

Timimoun, Algeria

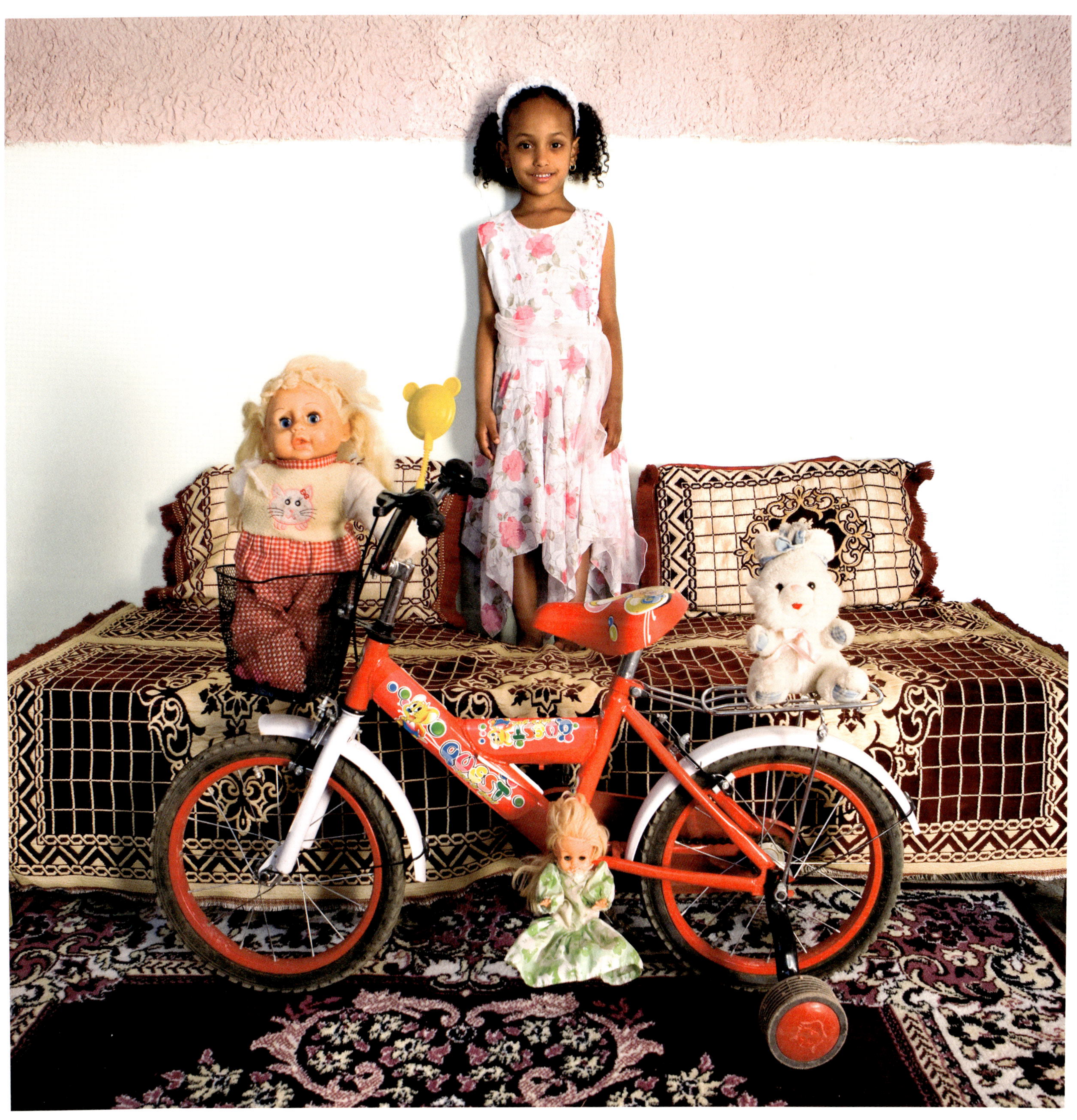
QUEST
QUEST

Oscar, 6

Bath, U.K.

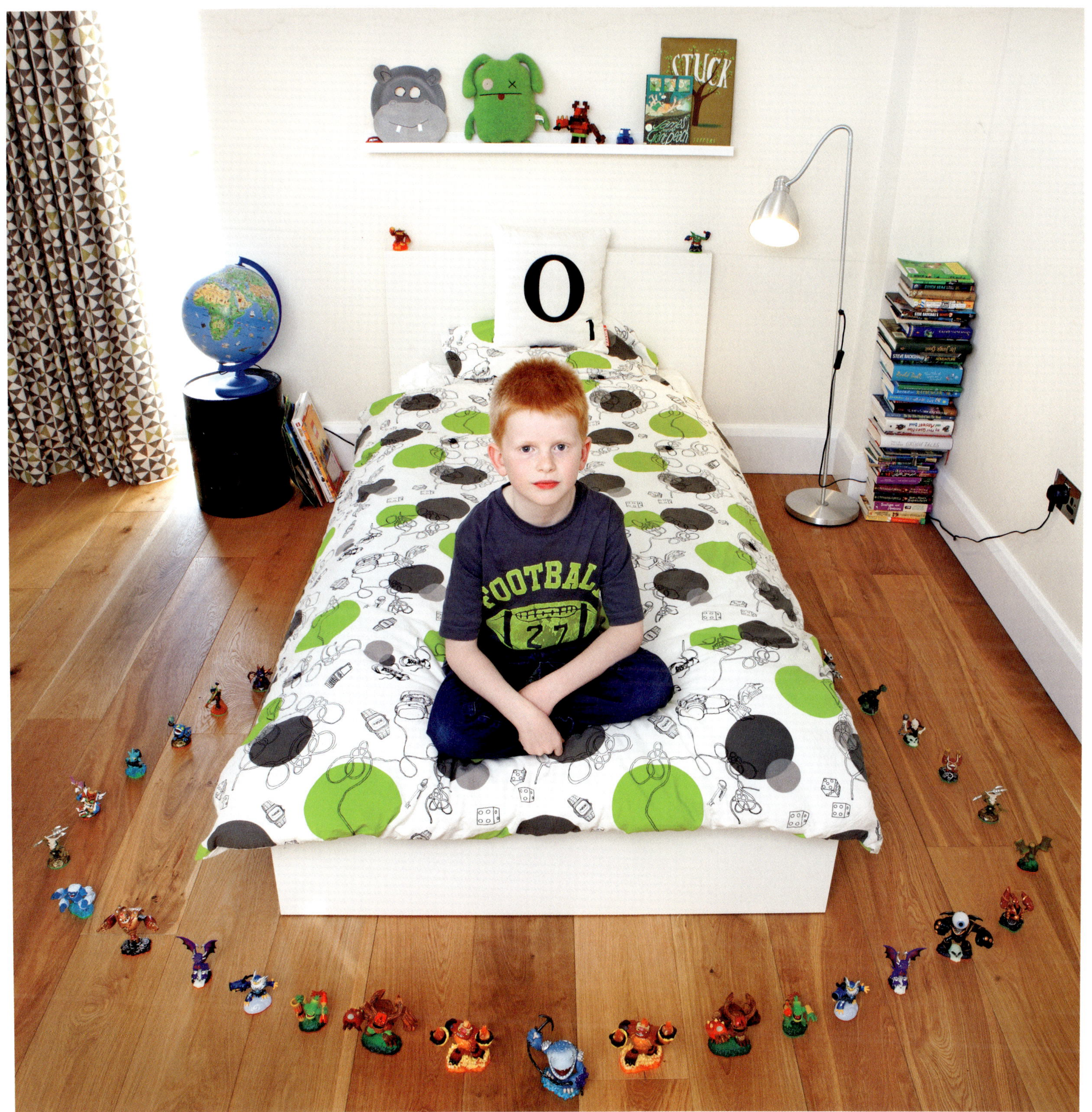
STUCK
27

Virginia, 4

American Fork, Utah

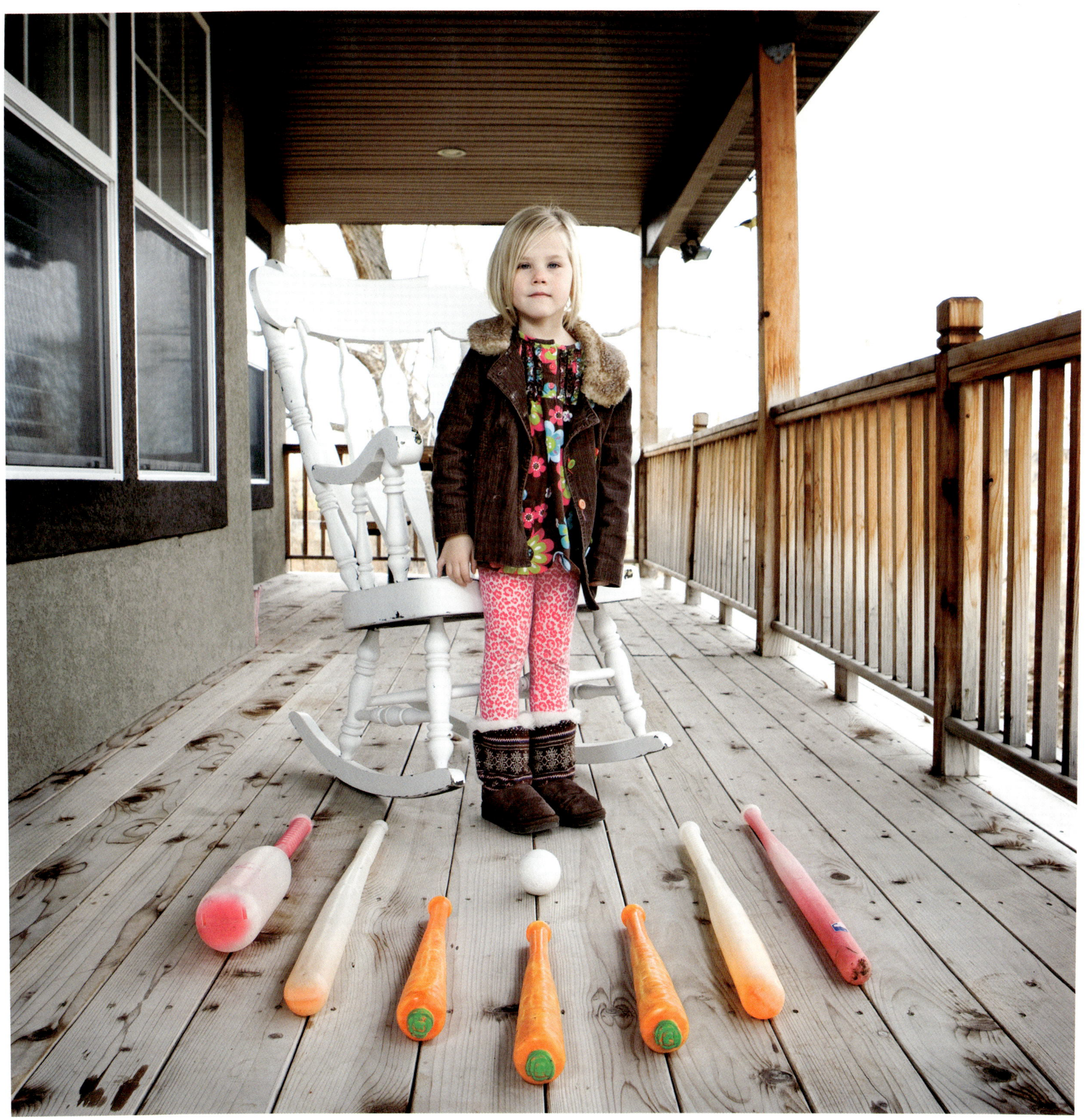

Watcharapon, 4

Bangkok, Thailand

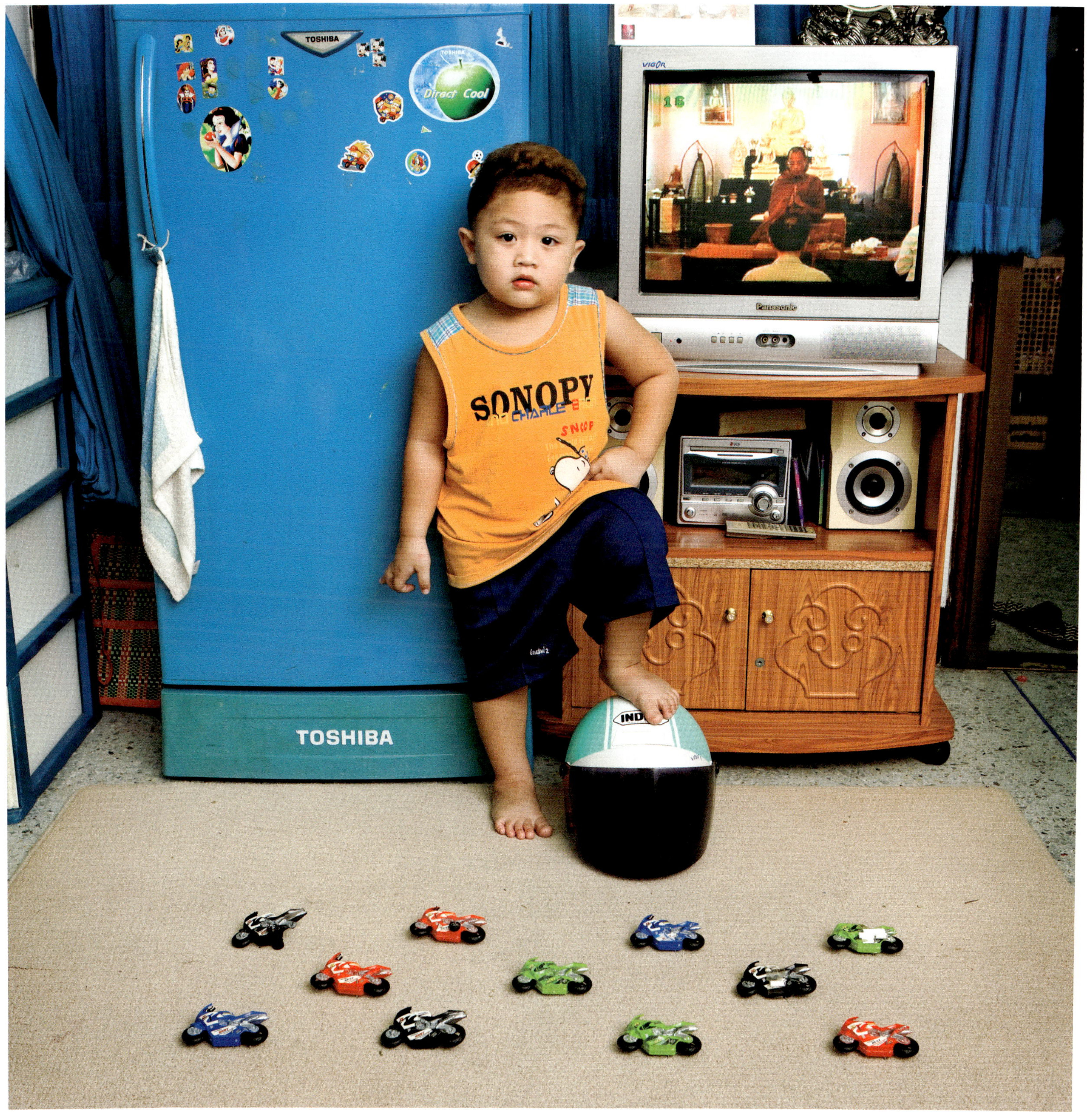
TOSHIBA
Direct Cool
Panasonic
SONOPY
TOSHIBA

Shaira, 6

Mumbai, India

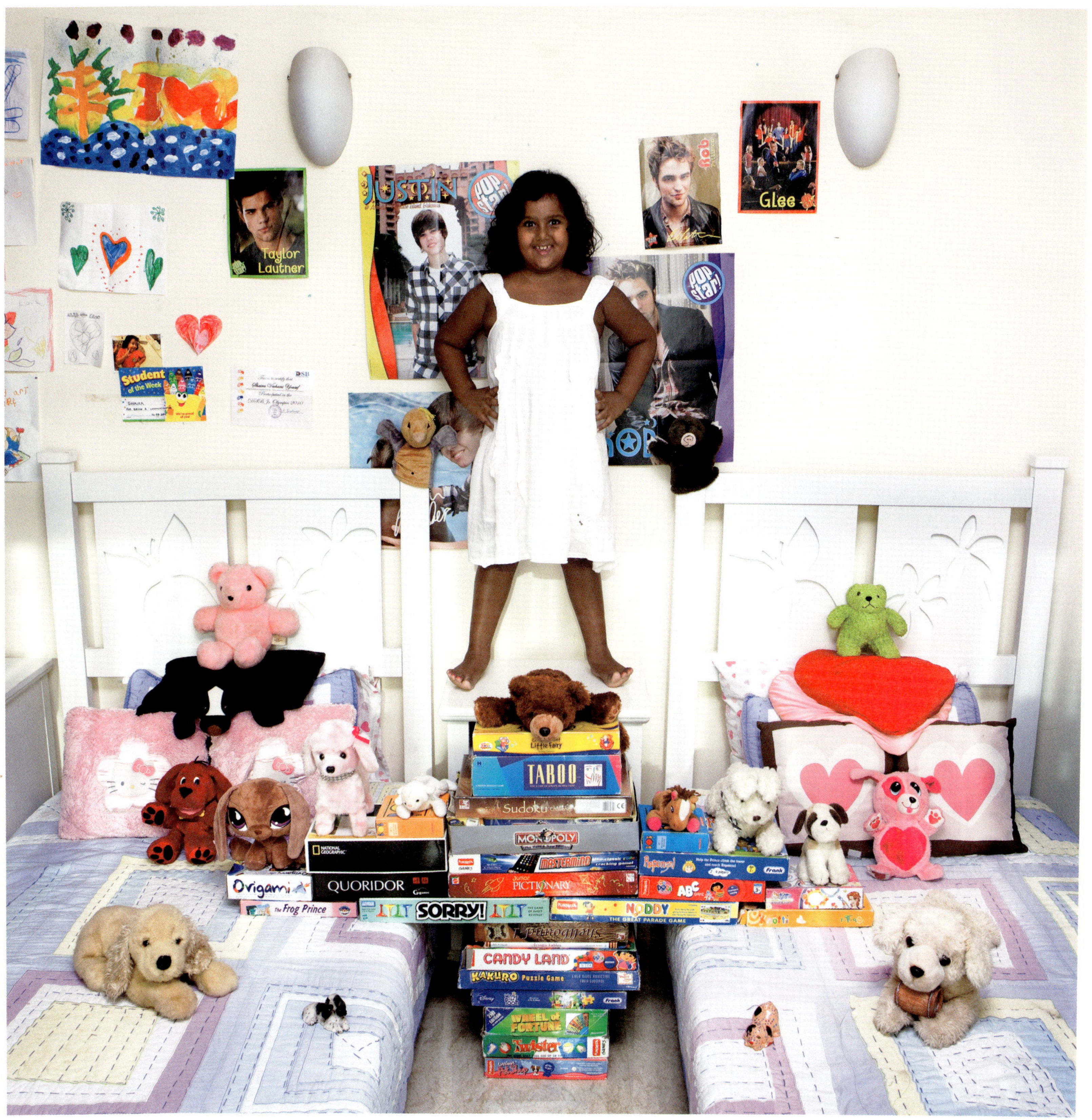
Taylor
Lauther
JUSTIN
POP star!
Rob
Glee
Student of the Week
TABOO
Sudoku
MONOPOLY
MASTERMIND
NATIONAL GEOGRAPHIC
QUORIDOR
Origami
The Frog Prince
SORRY!
Junior PICTIONARY
NODDY
THE GREAT PARADE GAME
ABC
CANDY LAND
KAKURO Puzzle Game
WHEEL of FORTUNE
Twister

Abel, 4

Nopaltepec, Mexico

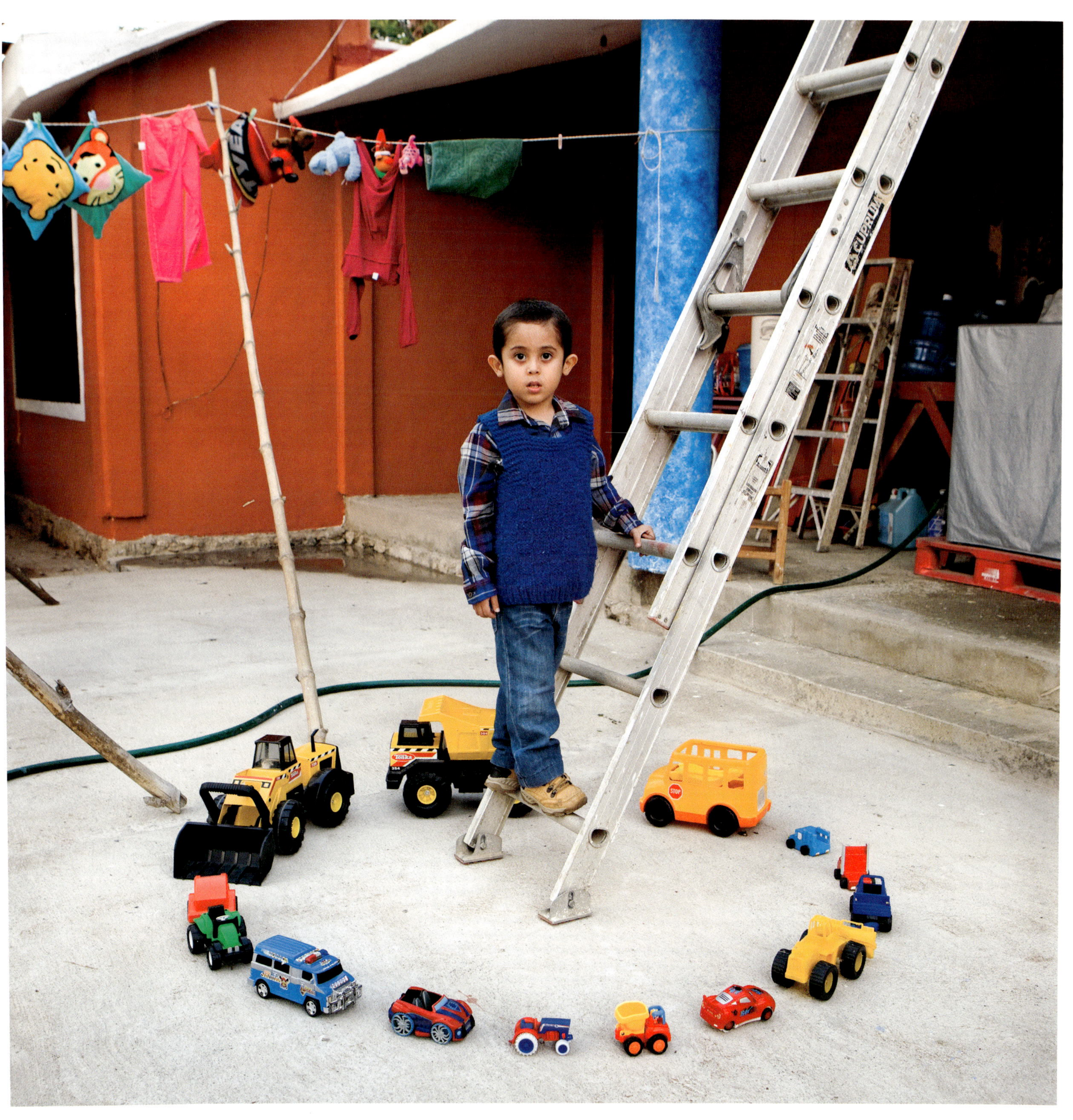
CUPRUM
Tonka
STOP

Roxane, 5

Paris, France

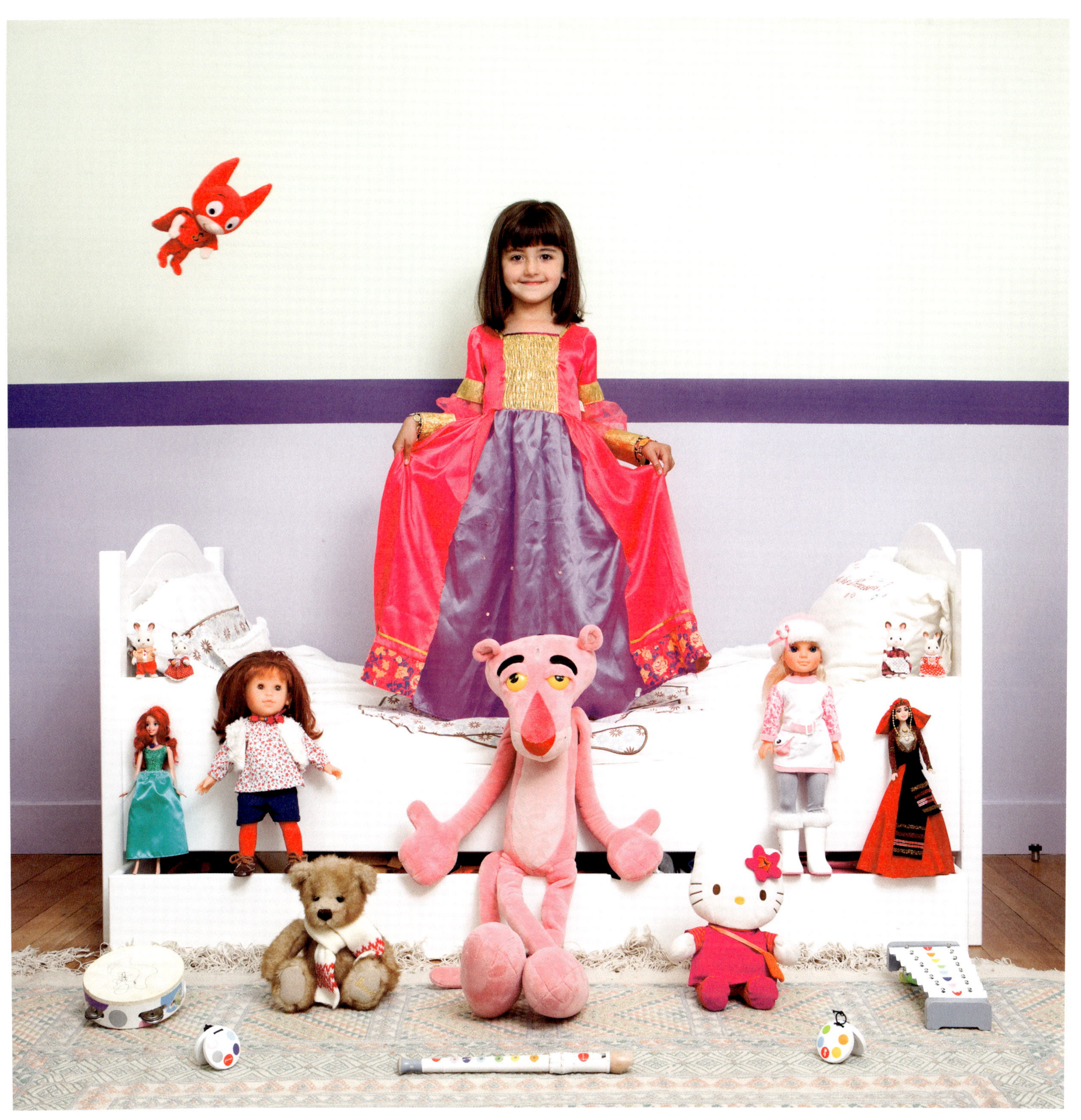

Enea, 3

Boulder, Colorado

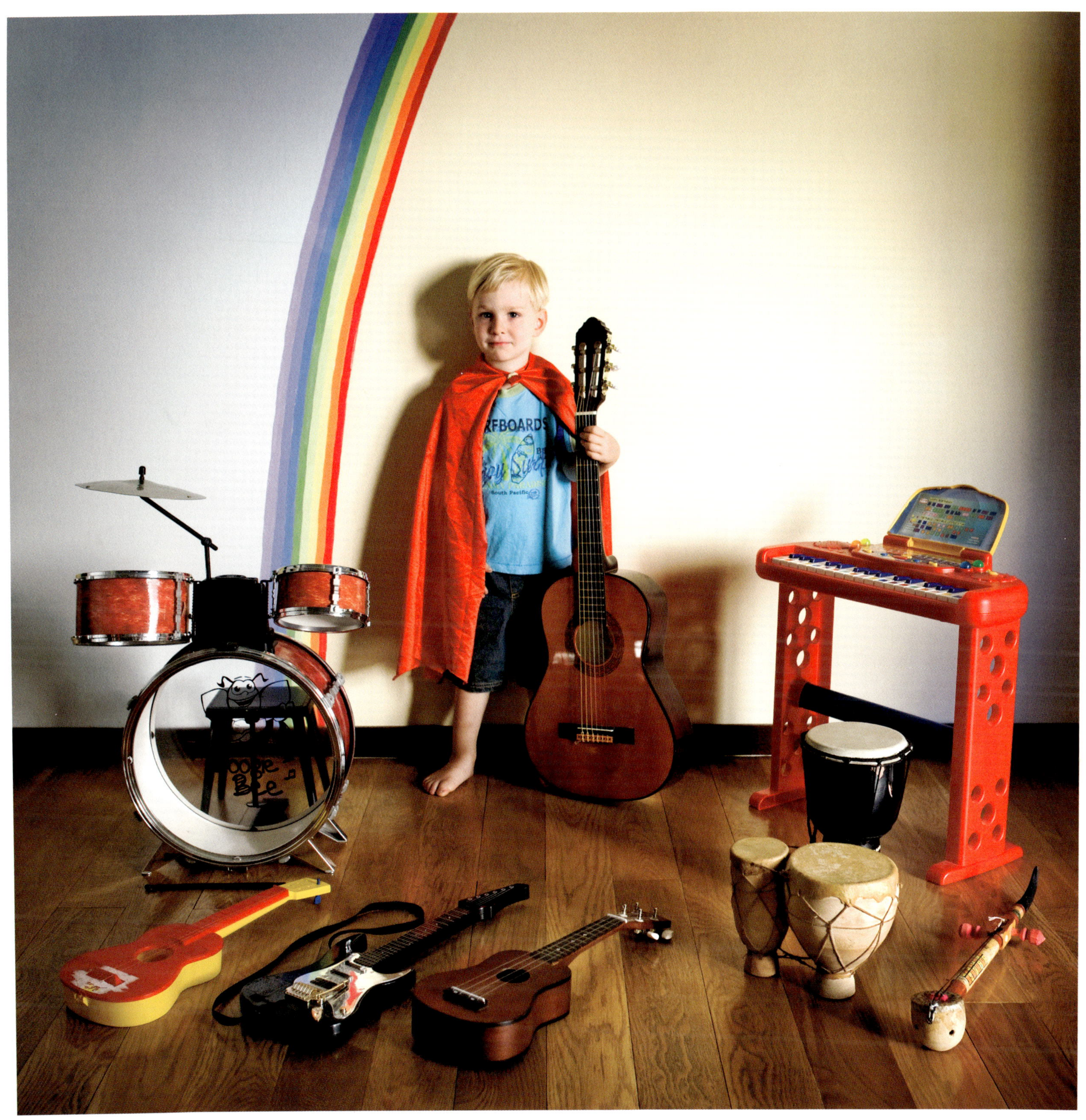
RFBOARDS
South Pacific

Farida, 4

Cairo, Egypt

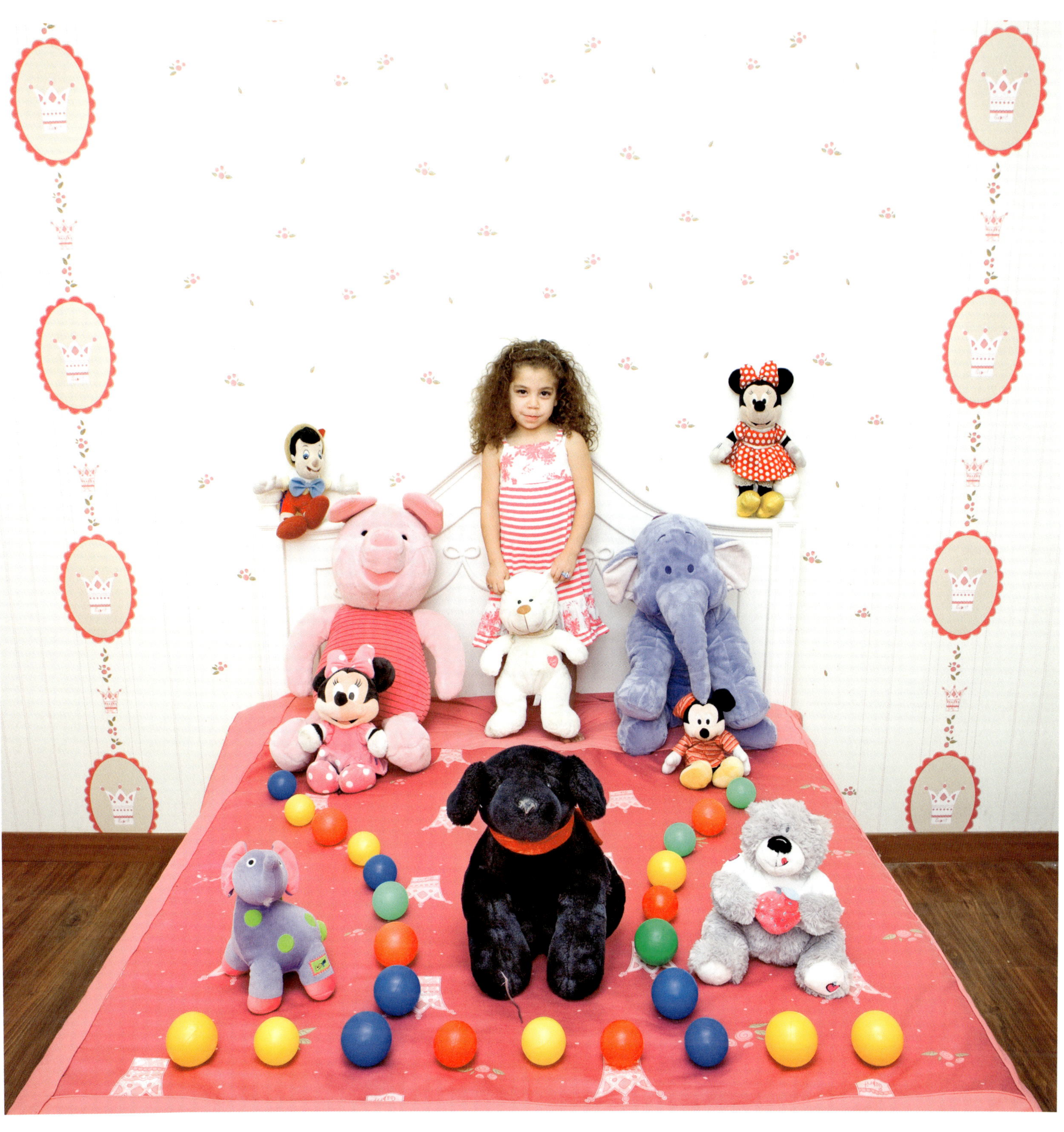

Louis, 4

Buena Vista, Colombia

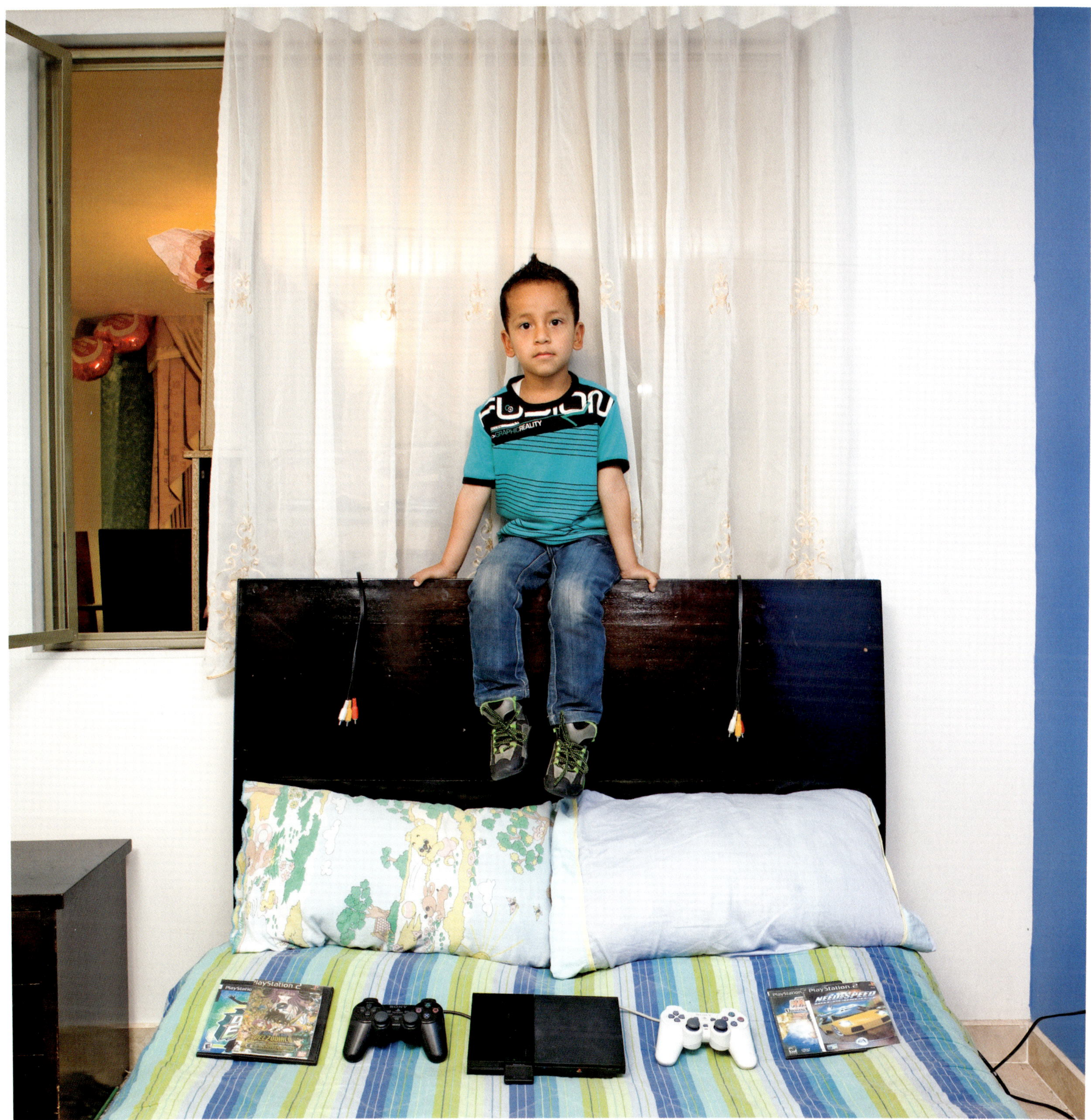
GRAPHIC REALITY
PlayStation 2
PlayStation 2
NEED FOR SPEED

Botlhe, 3

Maun, Botswana

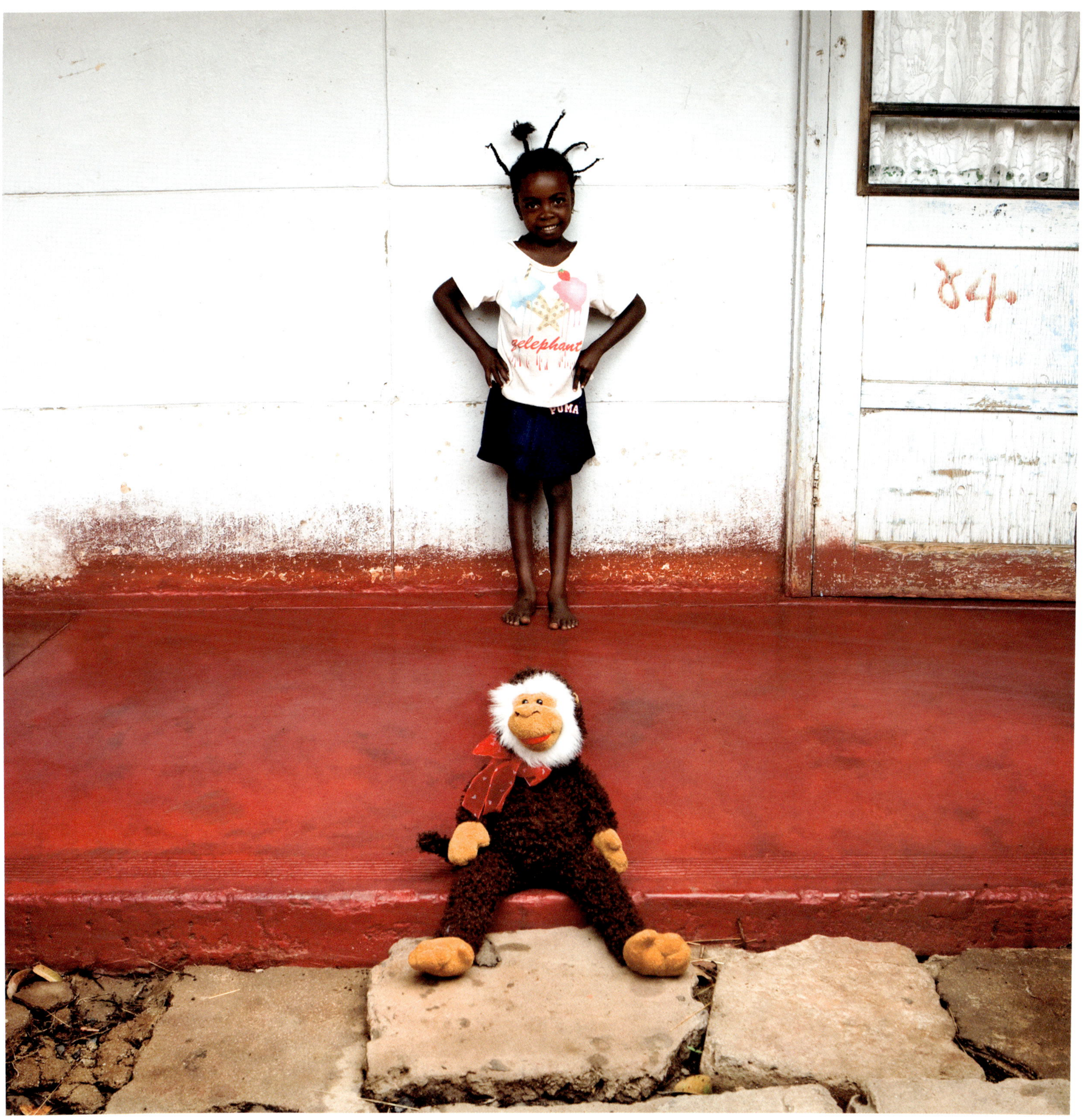
zelephant
PUMA

Ryan, 6

Johannesburg, South Africa

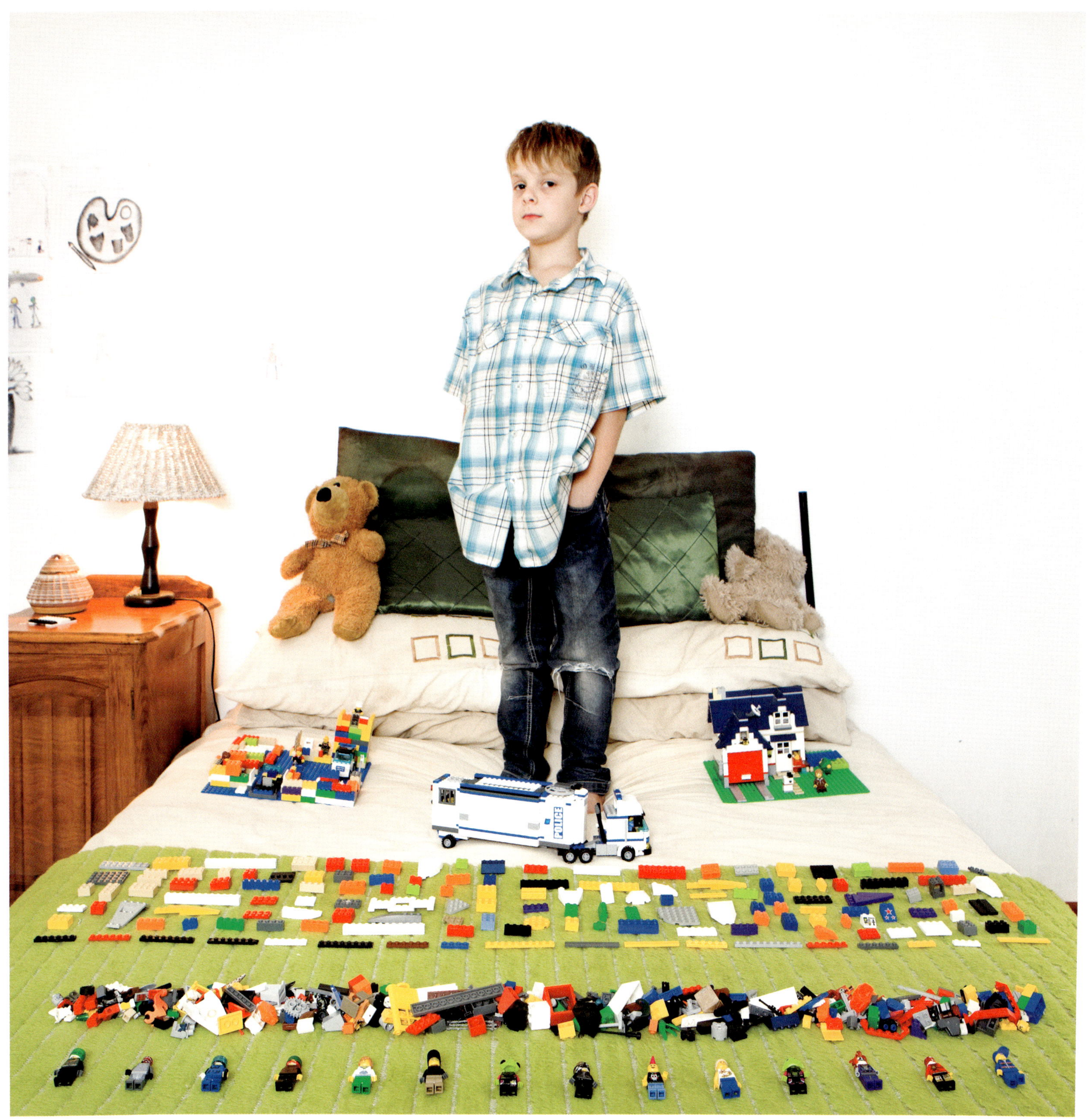
POLICE

Elene, 5

Tbilisi, Georgia

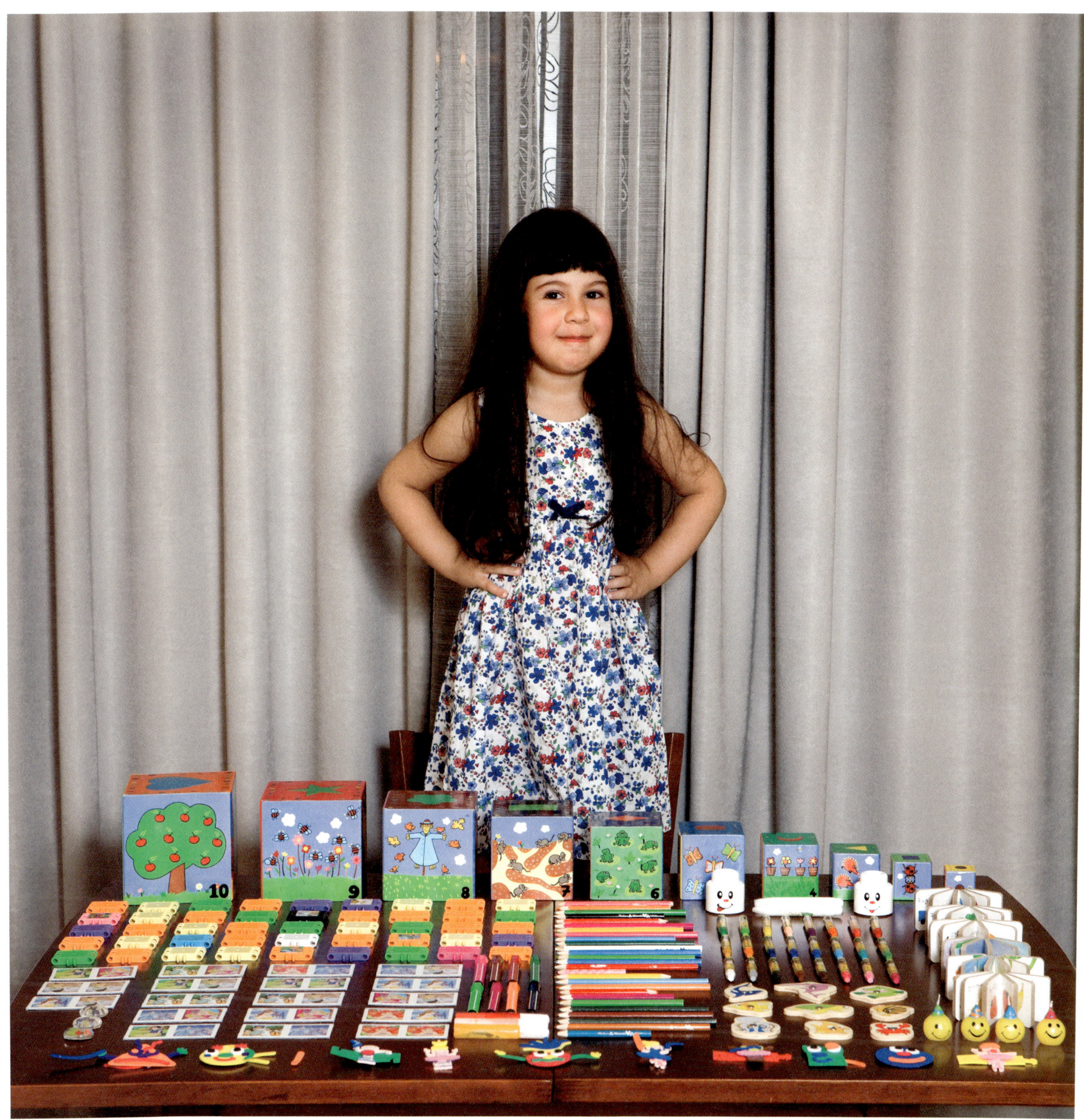
10
9
8
7
6
4

Niko, 5

Homer, Alaska

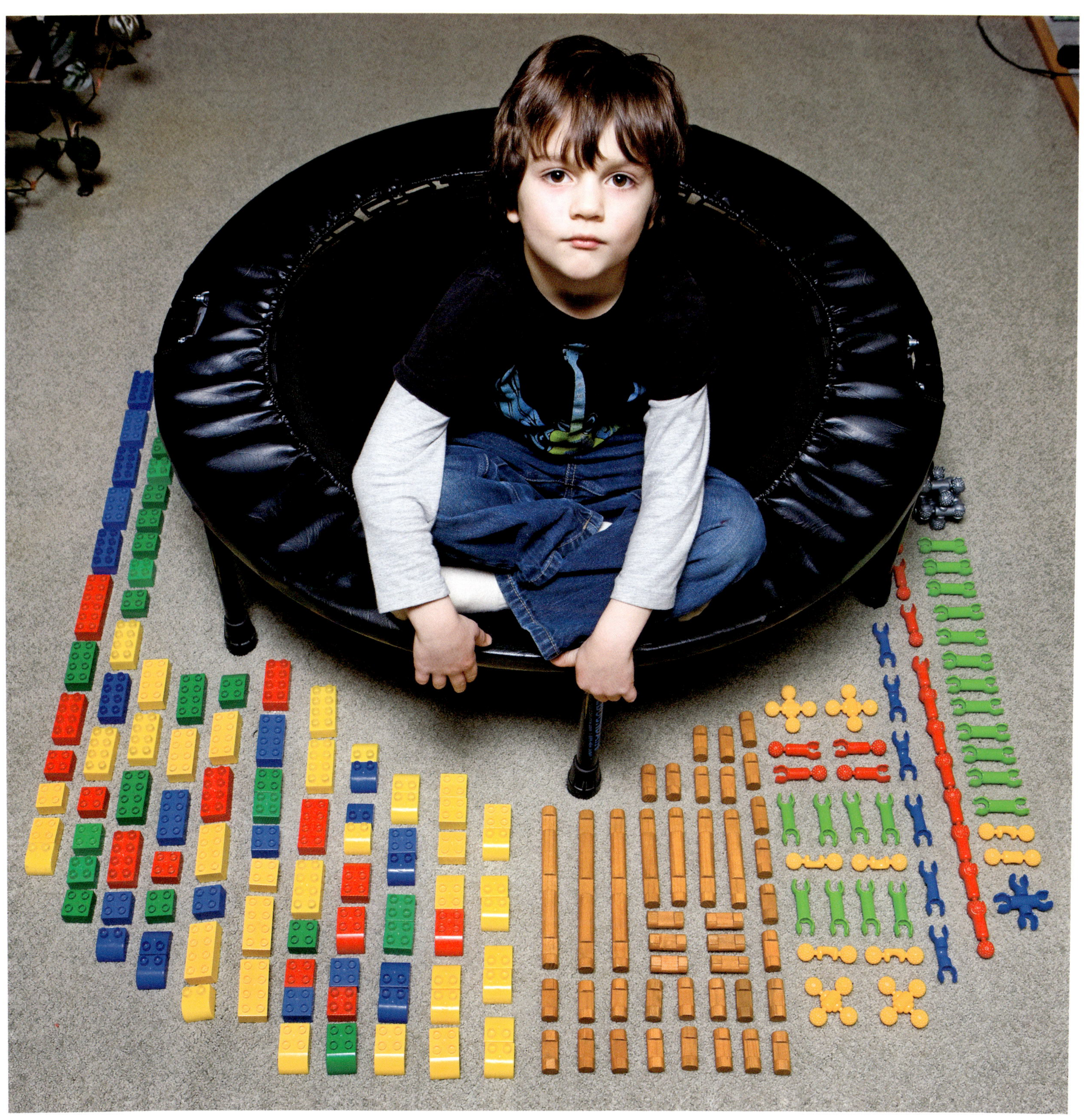

Fermina, 5

Montevideo, Uruguay

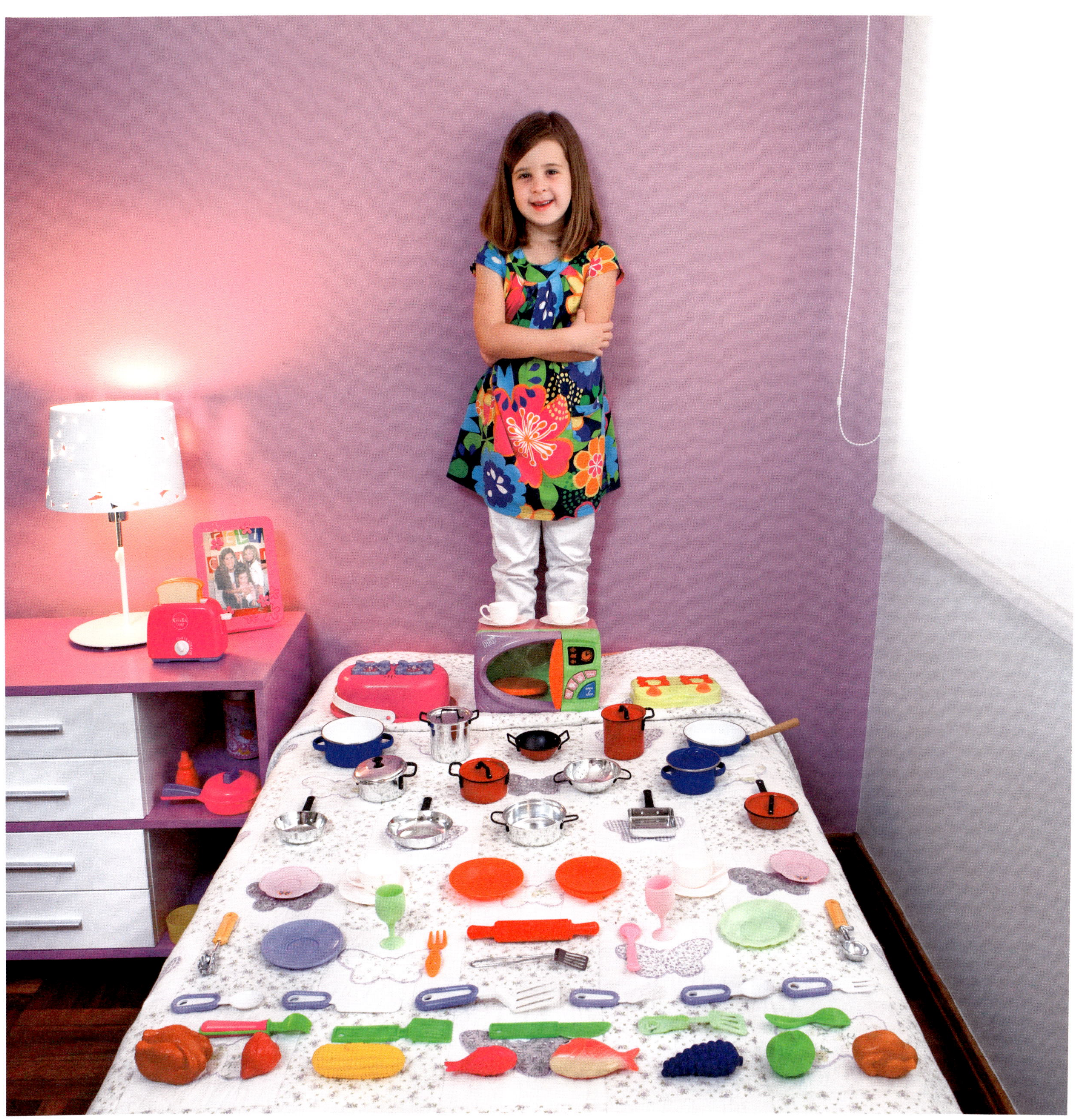

Norden, 4

Sidi Benzarne, Morocco

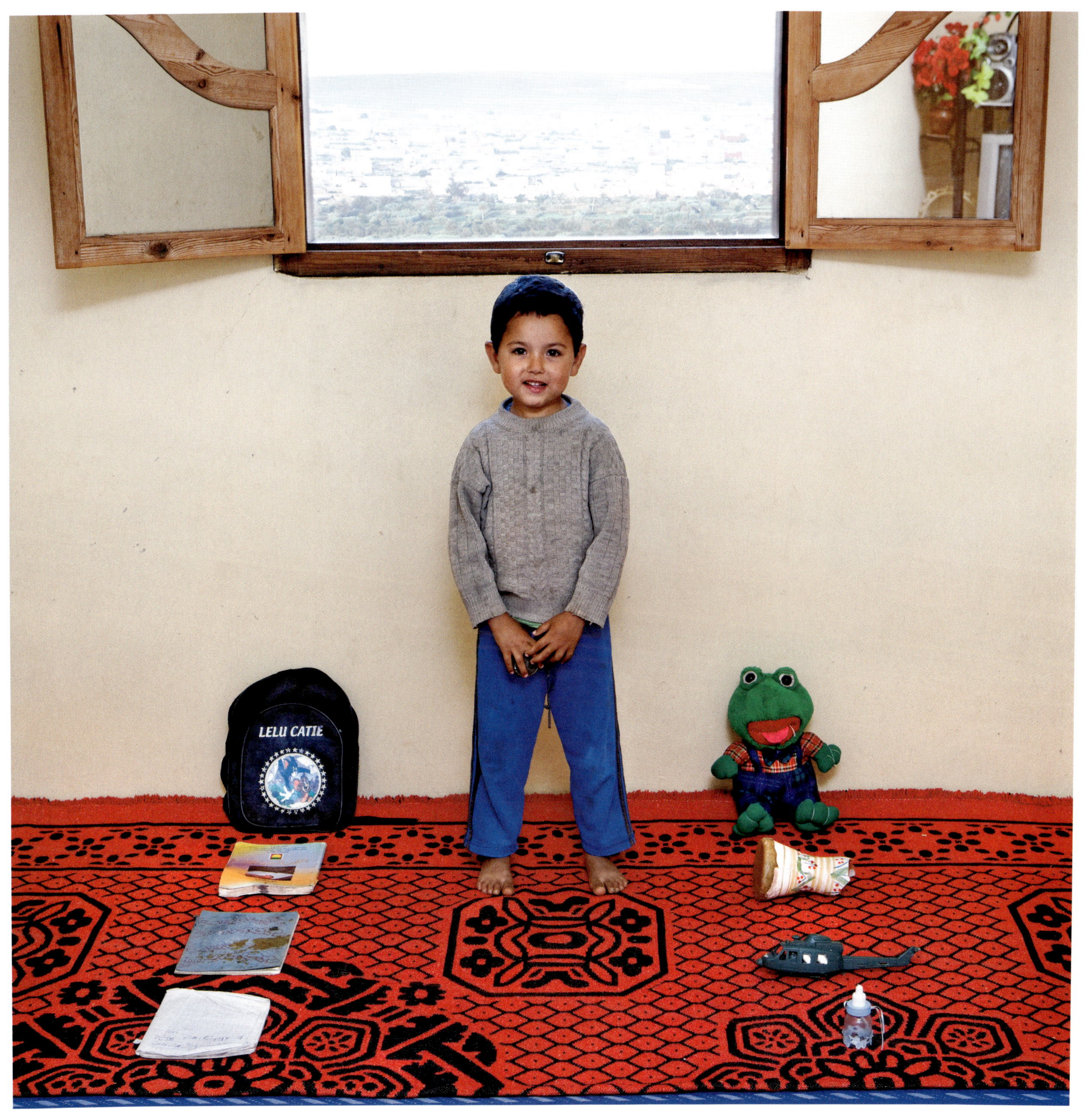
LELU CATIE

Alessia, 3

Castiglion Fiorentino, Italy

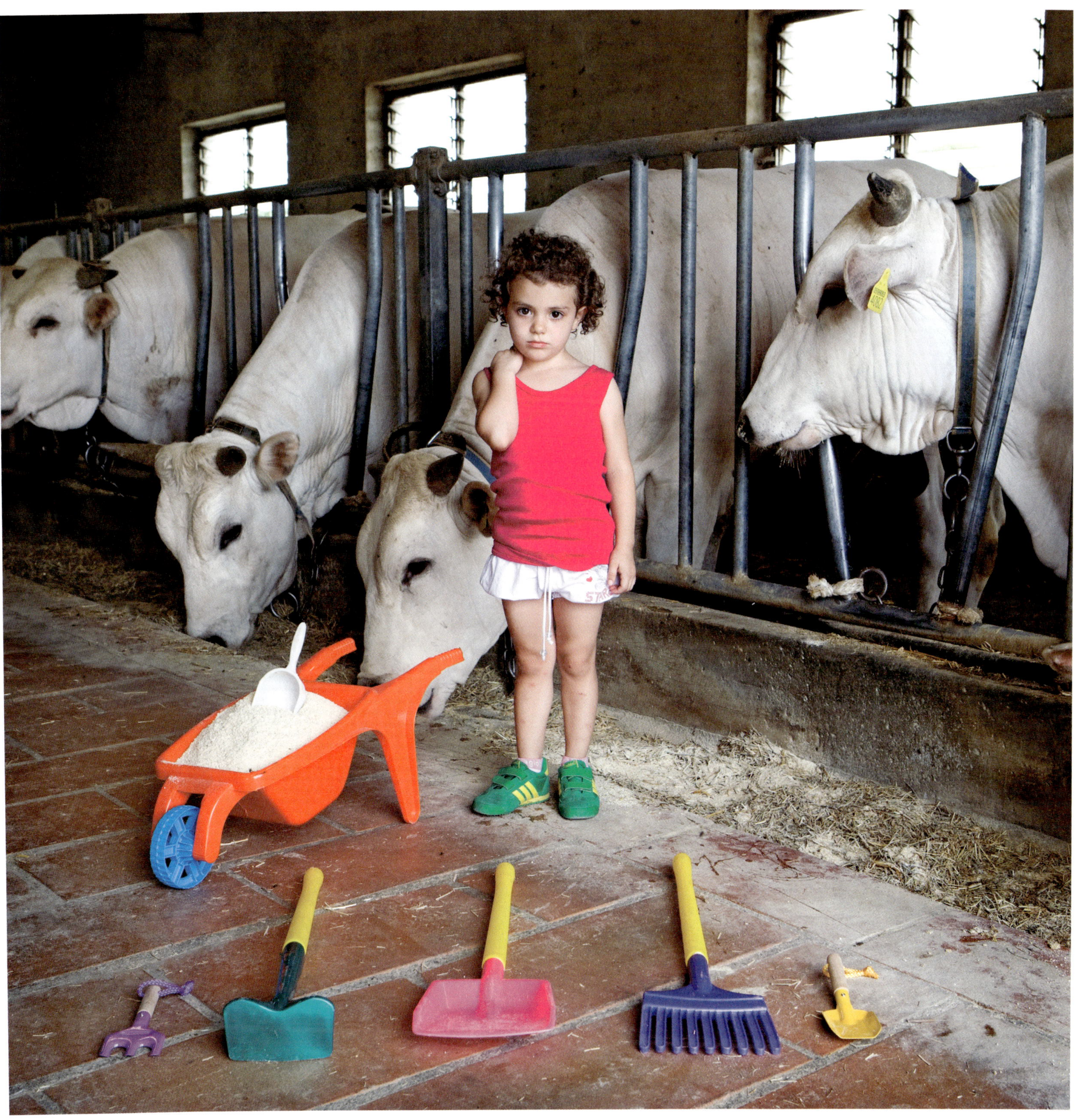

Noel, 5

Dallas, Texas

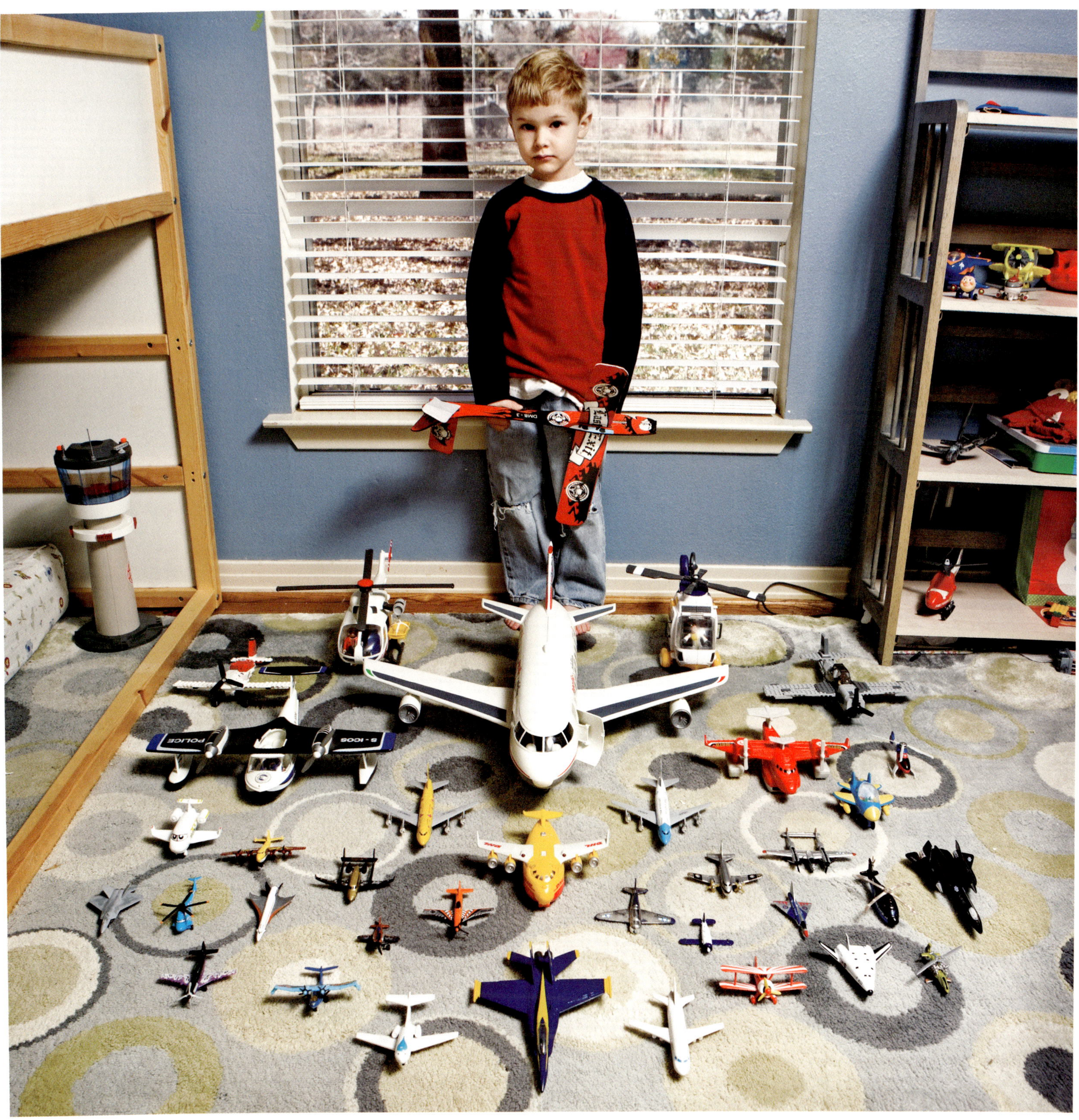
POLICE

Naya, 3

Puerto Viejo de Talamanca, Costa Rica

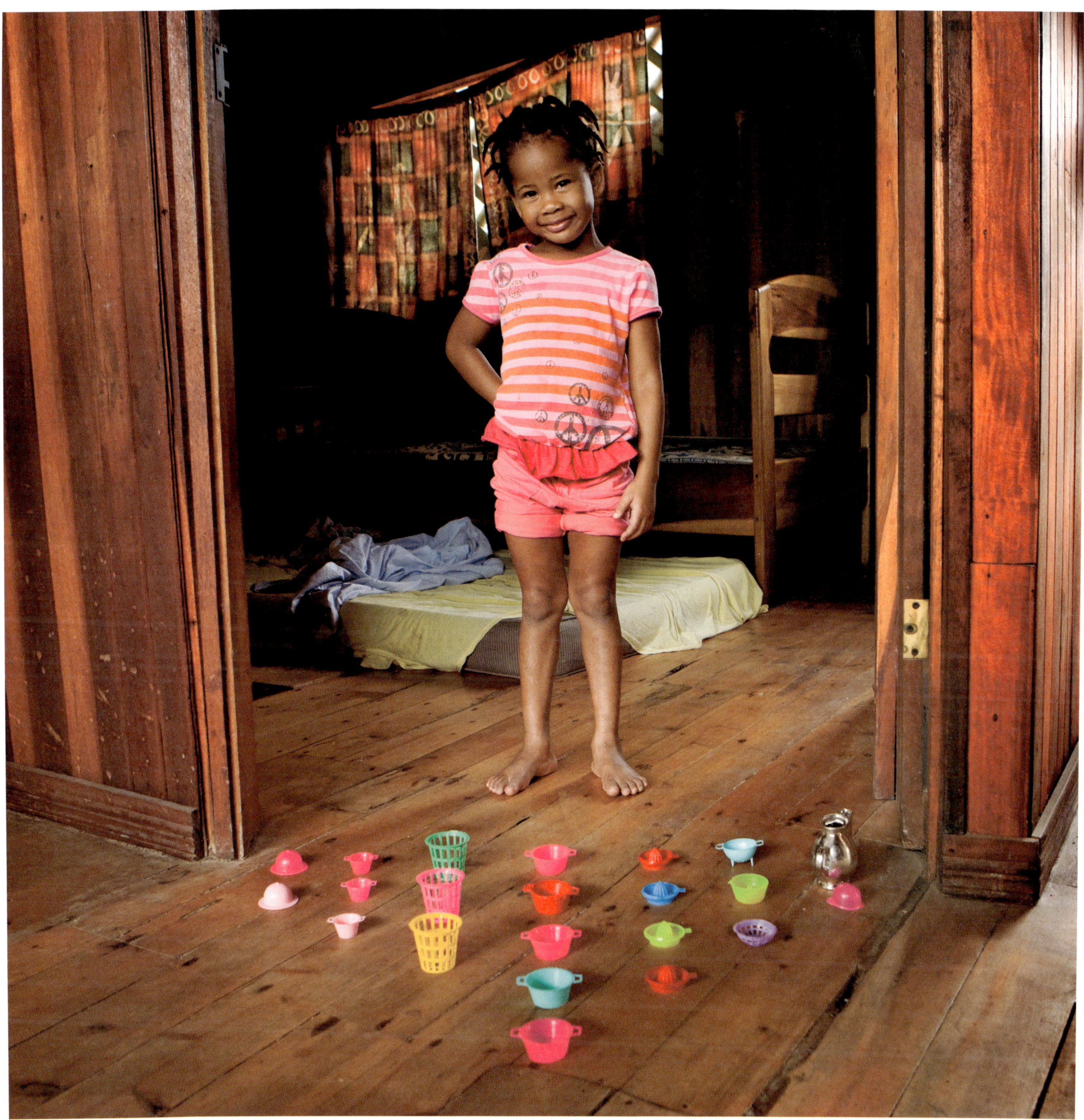

Gabriel, 3

Vila Madalena, Brazil

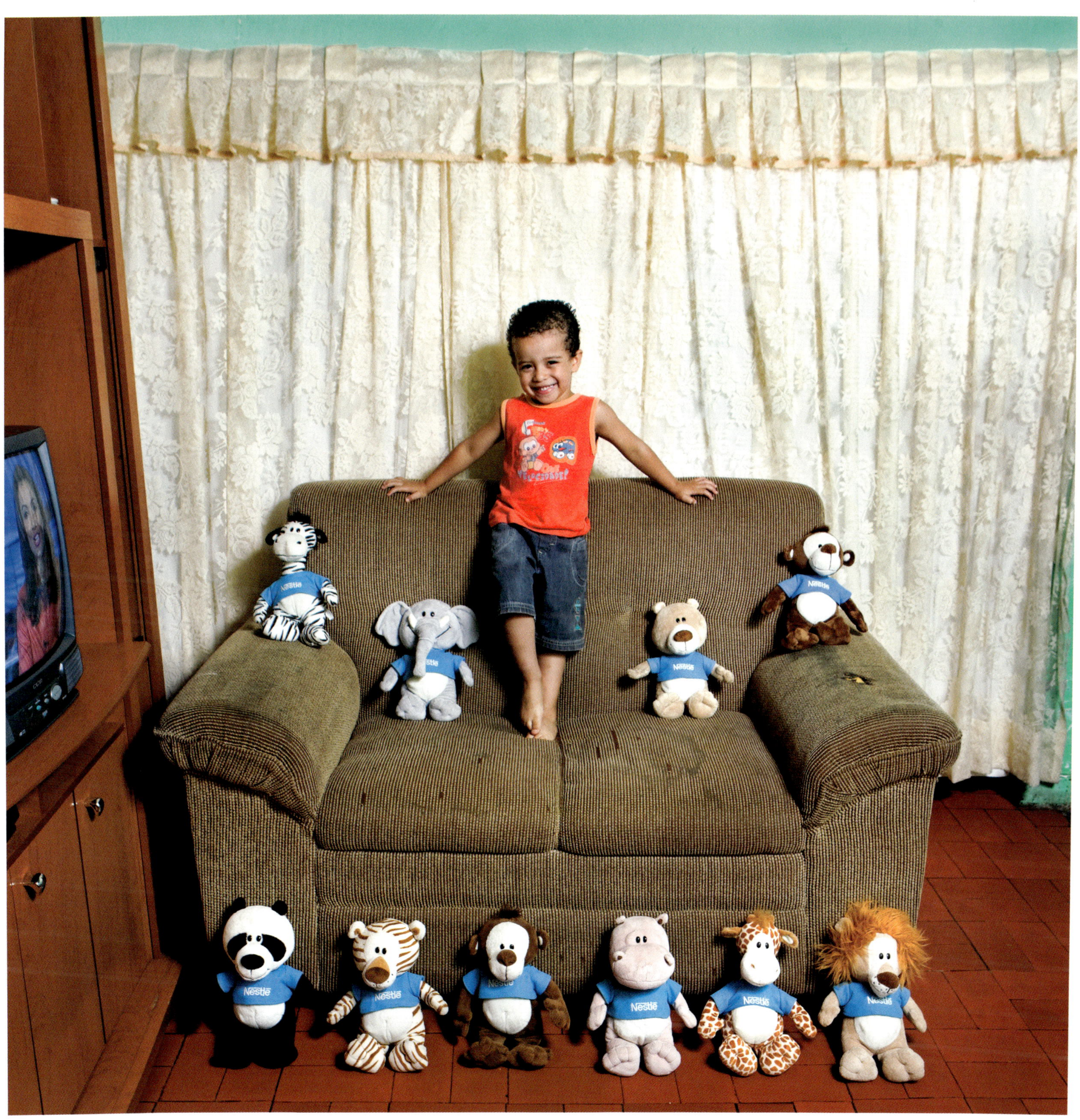
Nestlé

Sofia, 4

Bradford on Avon, U.K.

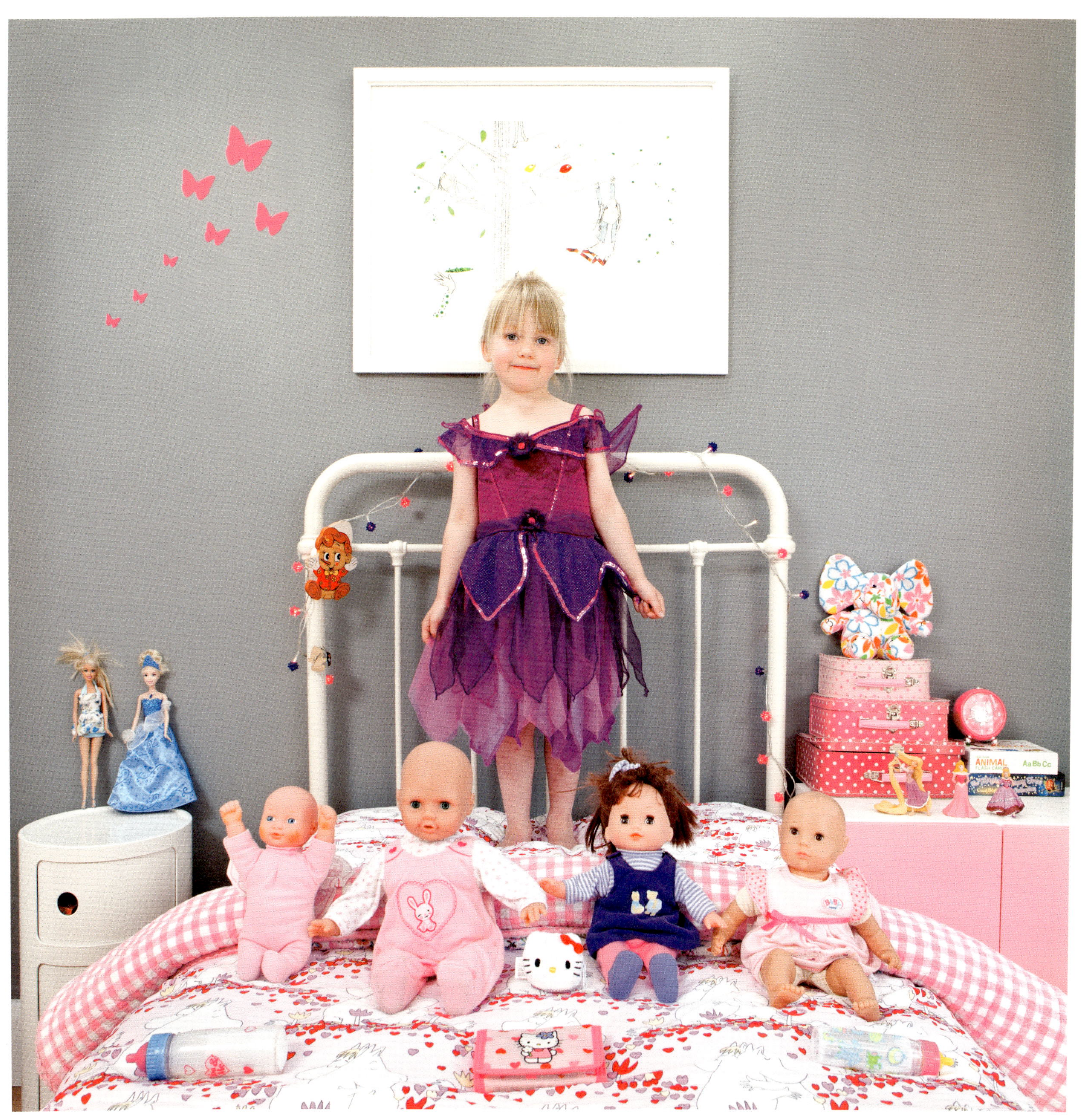
ANIMAL
AaBbCc

Pavel, 5

Kiev, Ukraine

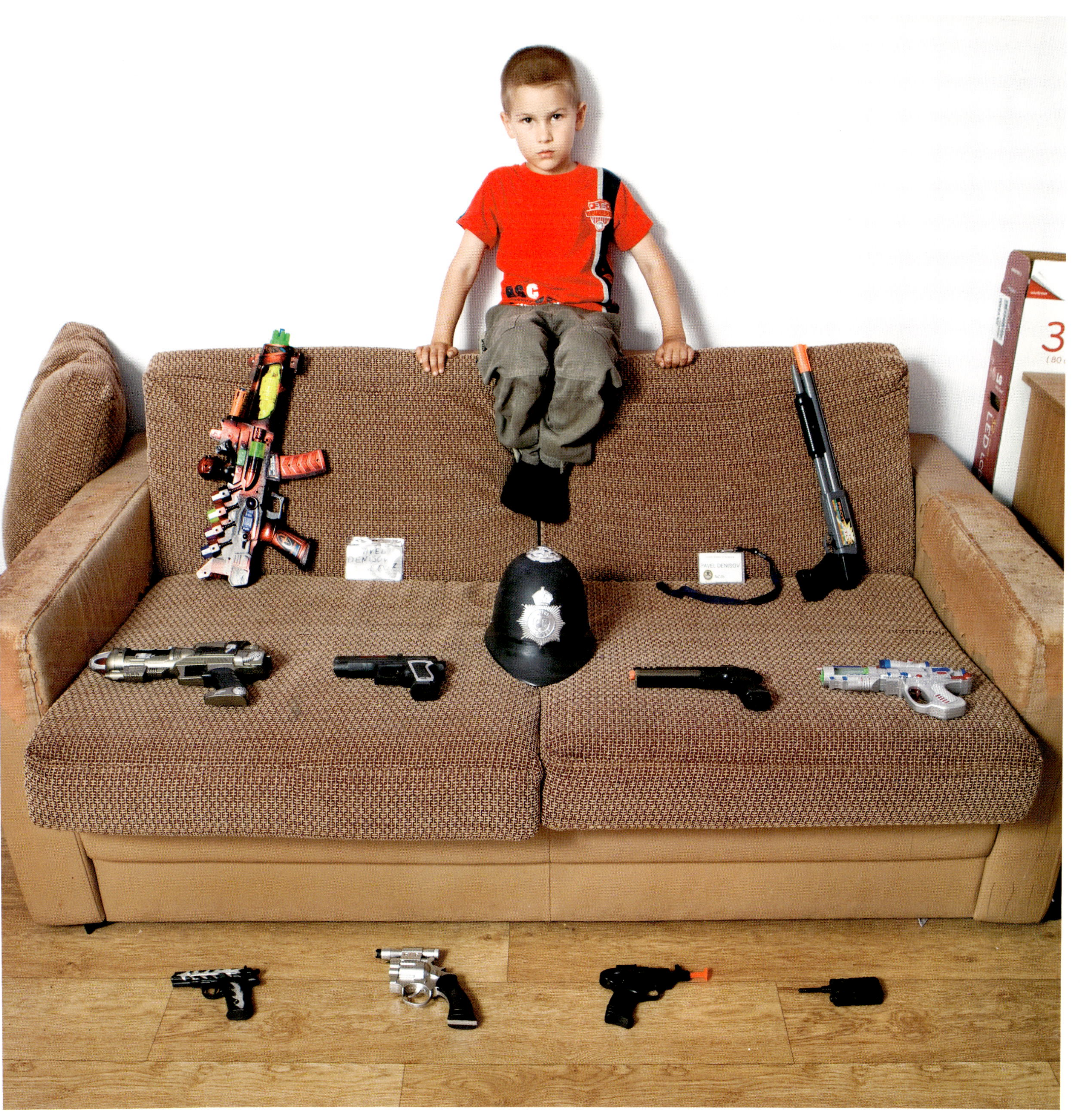
PAVEL DENISOV

Puput, 4

Ubud, Bali

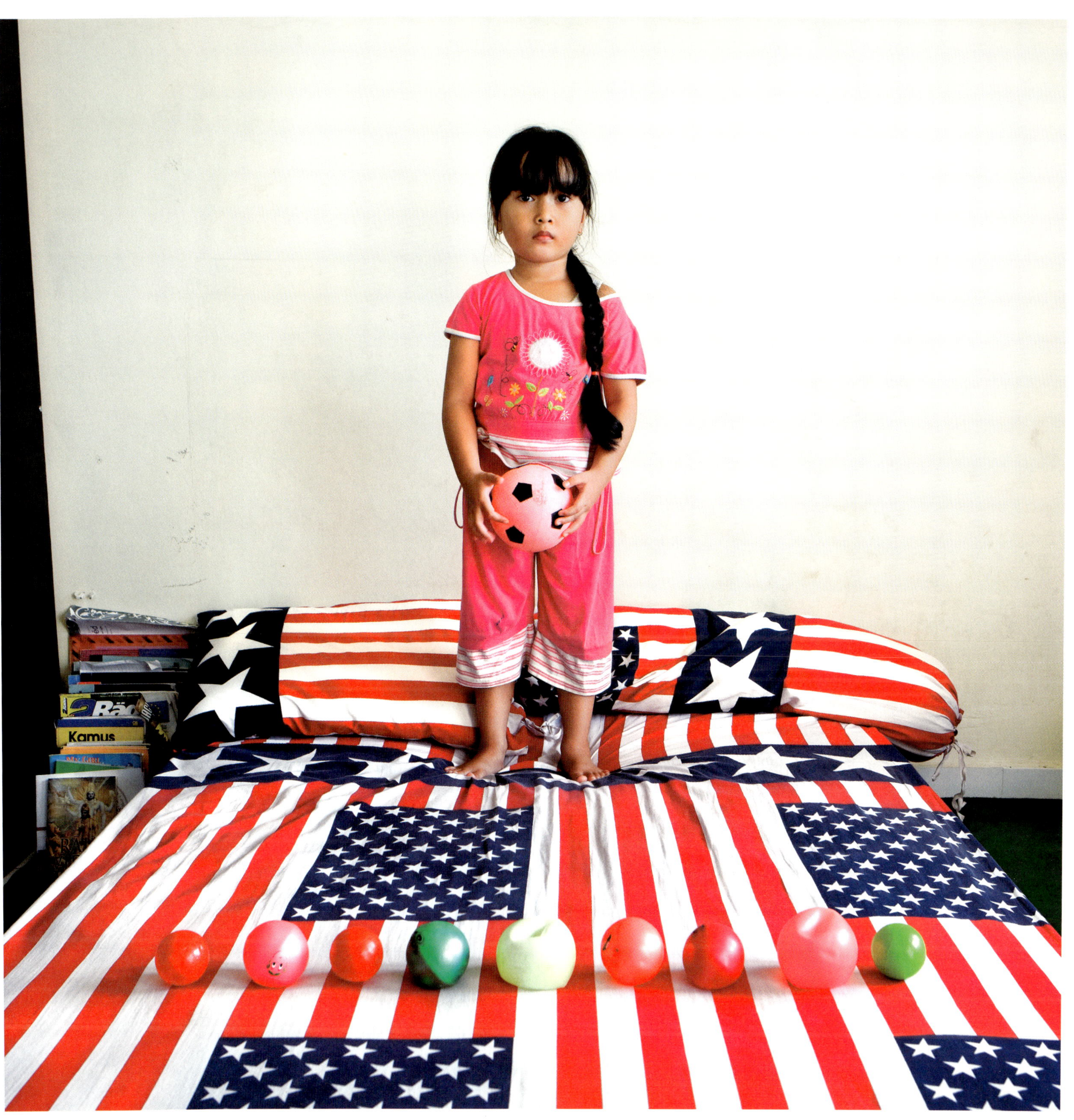
Kamus

Davide, 5

Valletta, Malta

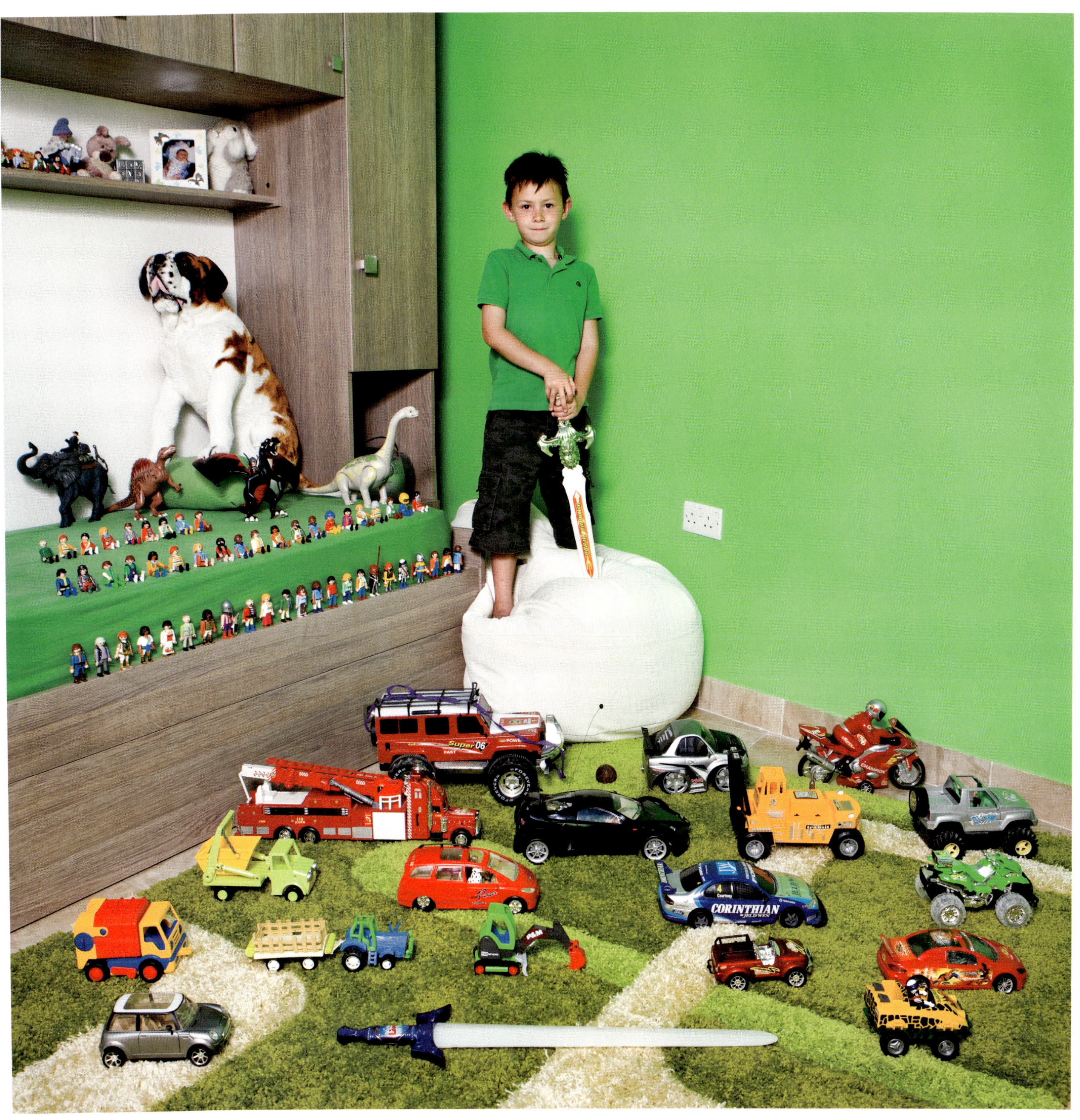
Super 06
CORINTHIAN

Lauren, 6

Muskoka, Canada

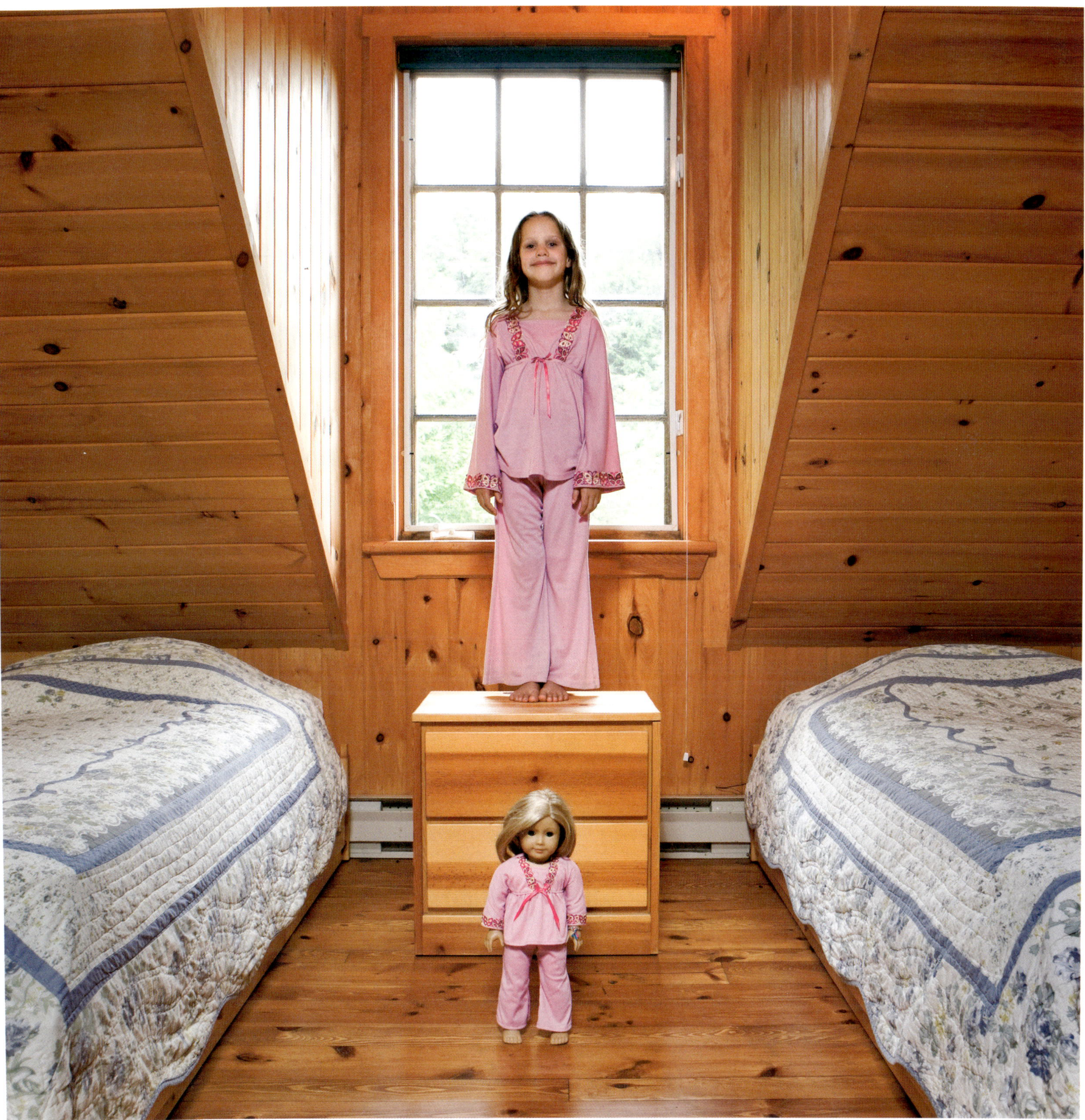

Jeronimo, 4

Bogotà, Colombia

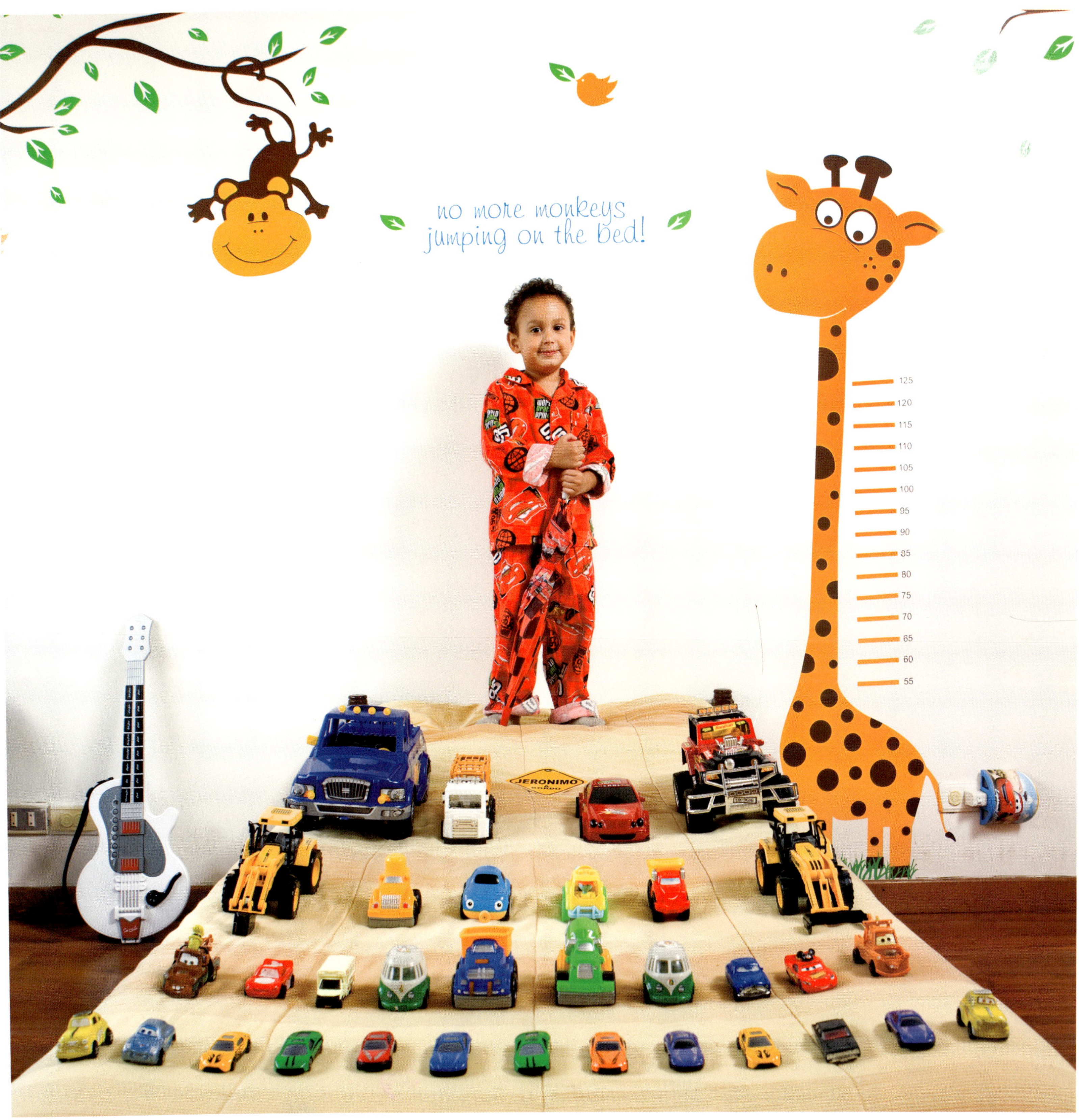
no more monkeys
jumping on the bed!
125
120
115
110
105
100
95
90
85
80
75
70
65
60
55
JERONIMO

Kalesi, 3

Viseisei, Fiji

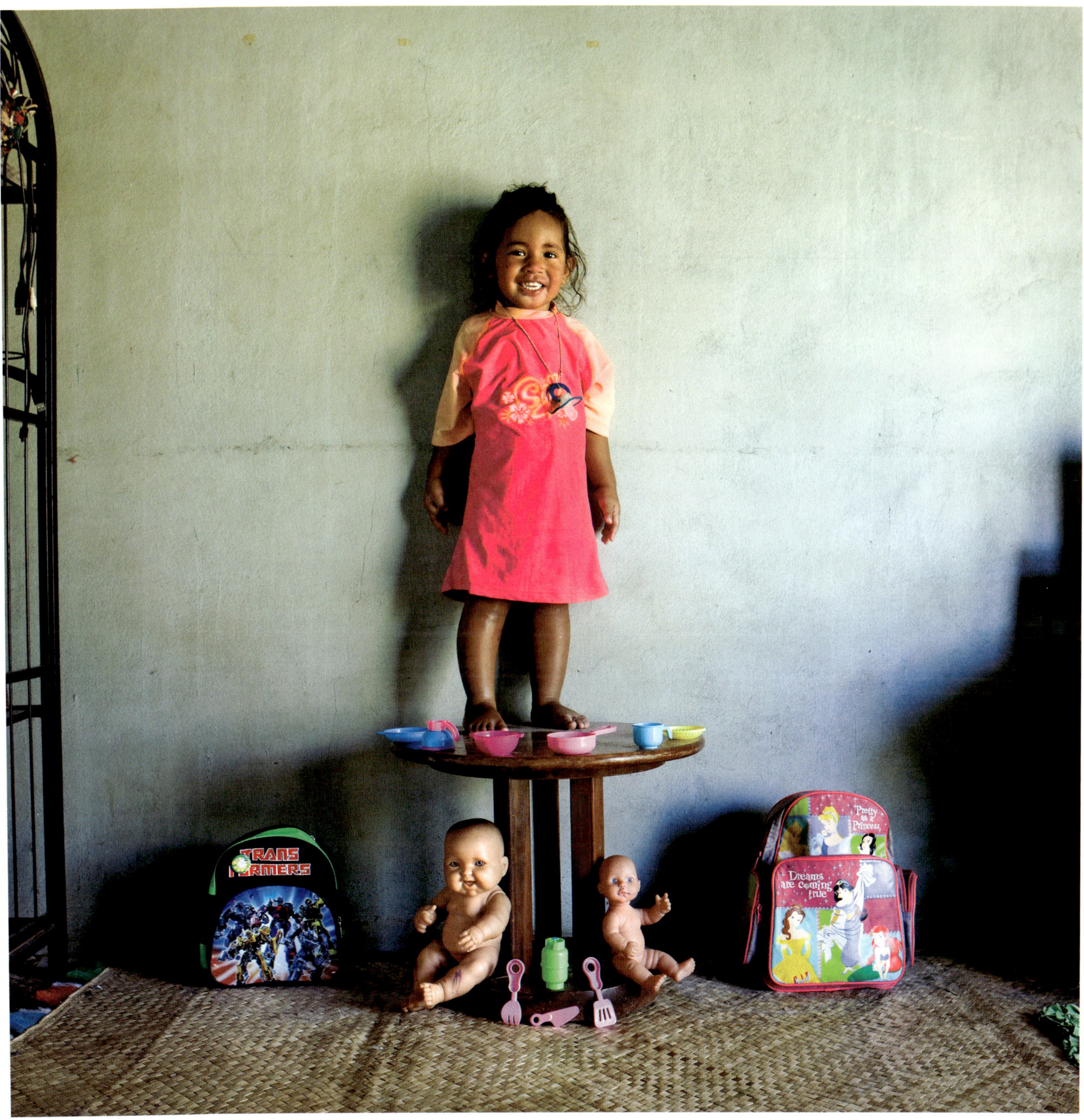
TRANS
Pretty
Princess
Dreams are coming true

Ralf, 4

Riga, Latvia

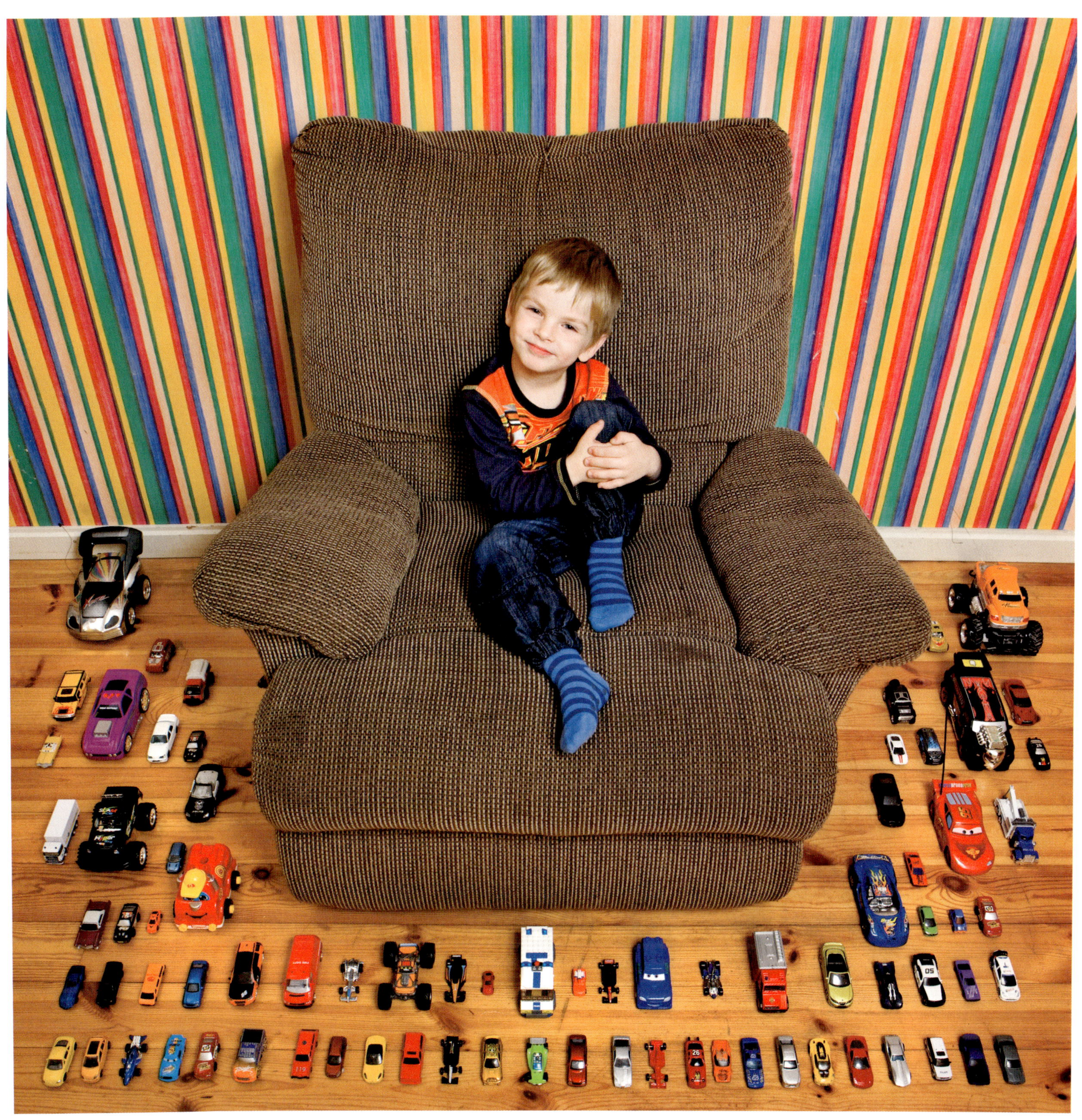

Stella, 4

Montecchio, Italy

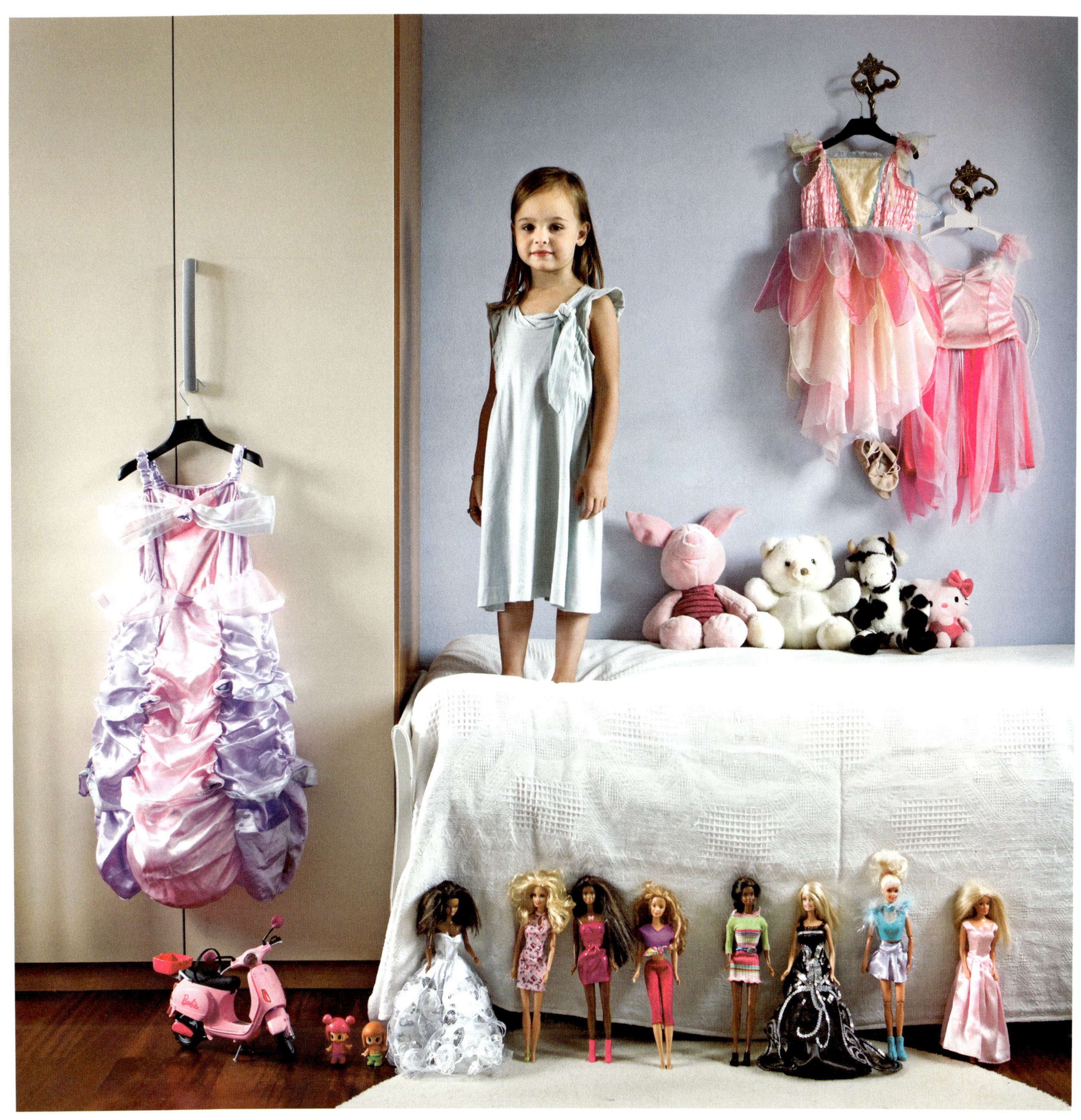
Barbie

Chiwa, 4

Mchinji, Malawi

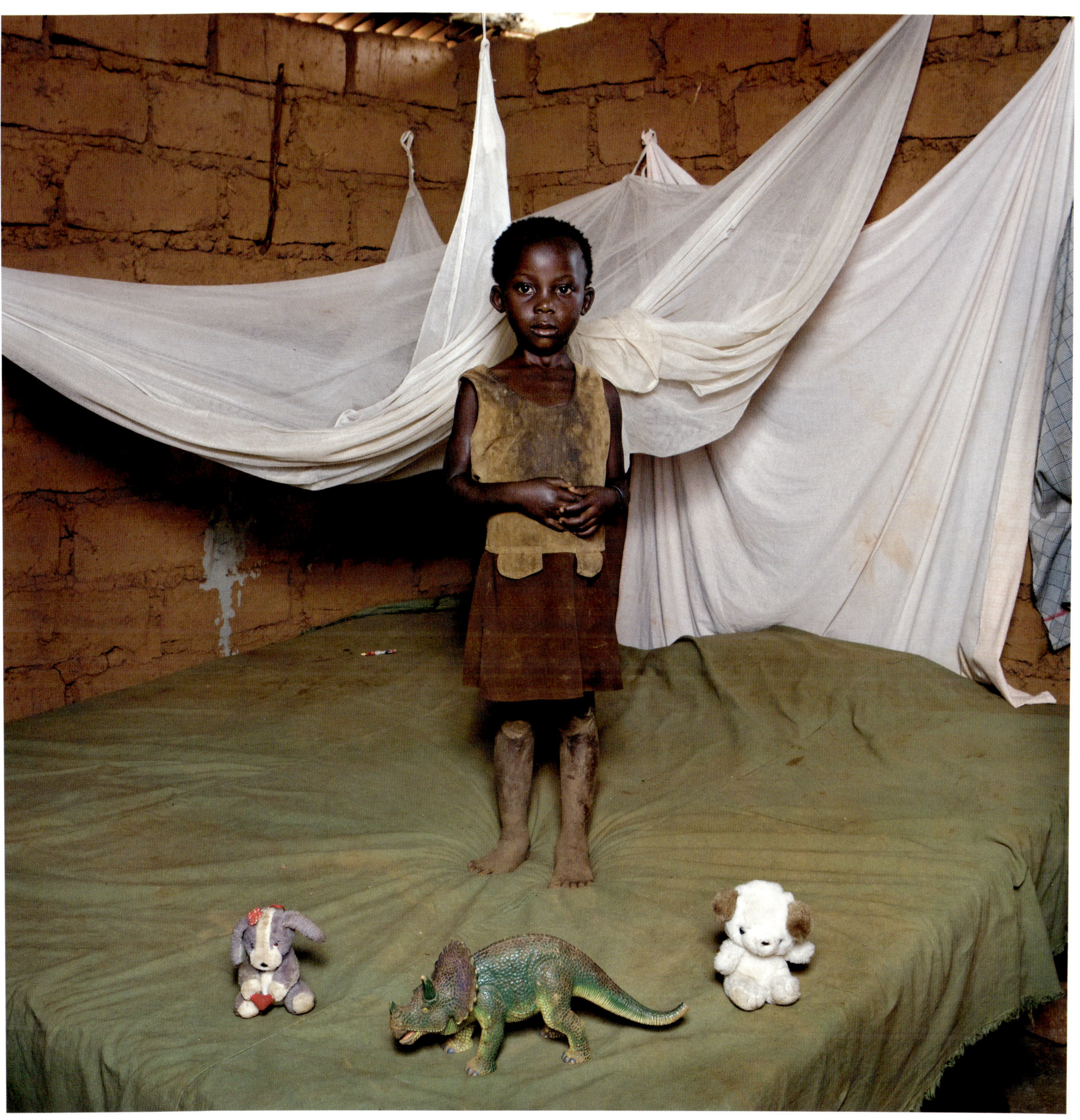

Luc, 3

São Paulo, Brazil

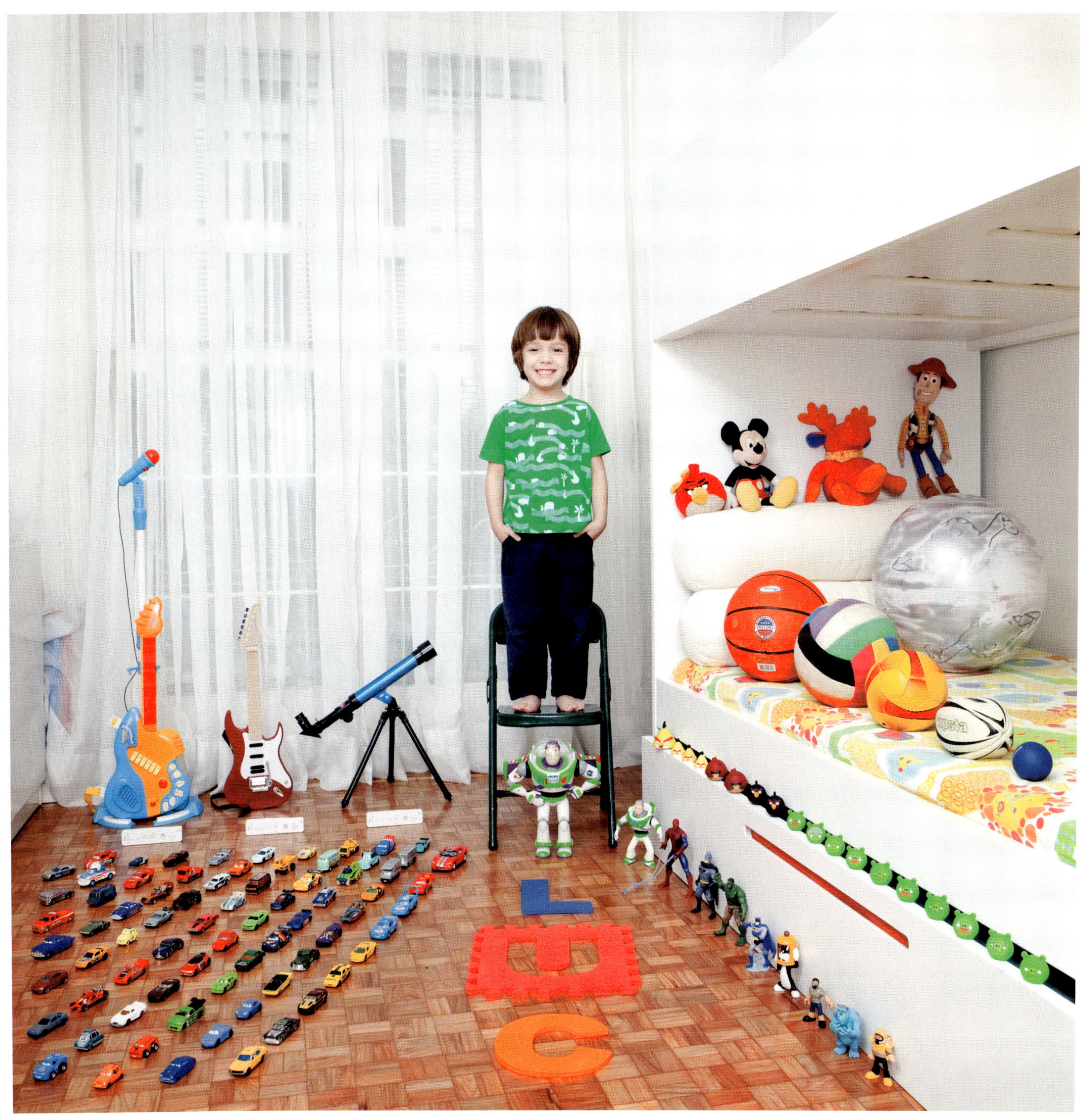

Lola, 3

Mendoza, Argentina

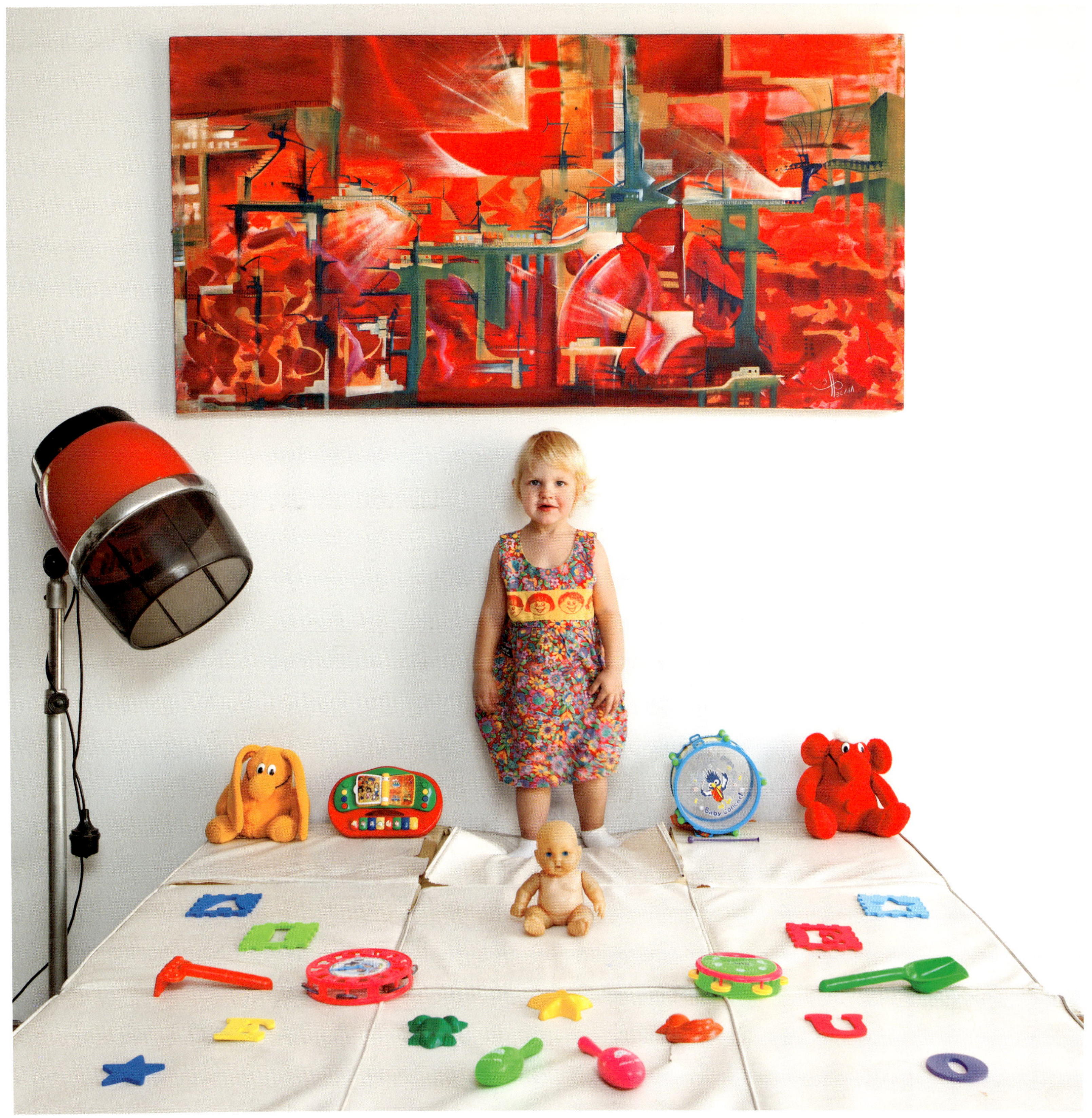
Baby Concert

Ragnar, 3

Reykjavik, Iceland

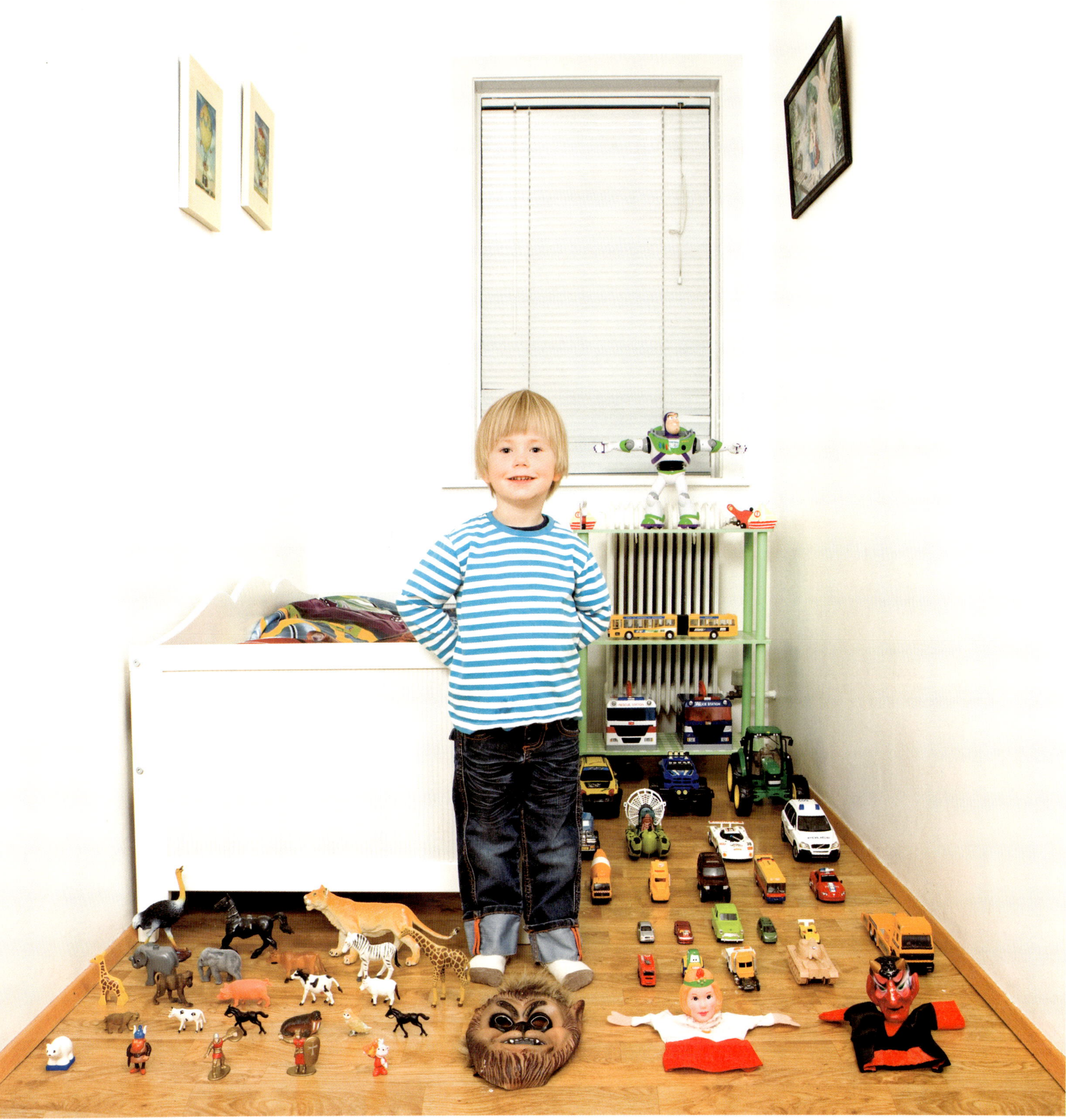

Ivi, 3

La Paz, Bolivia

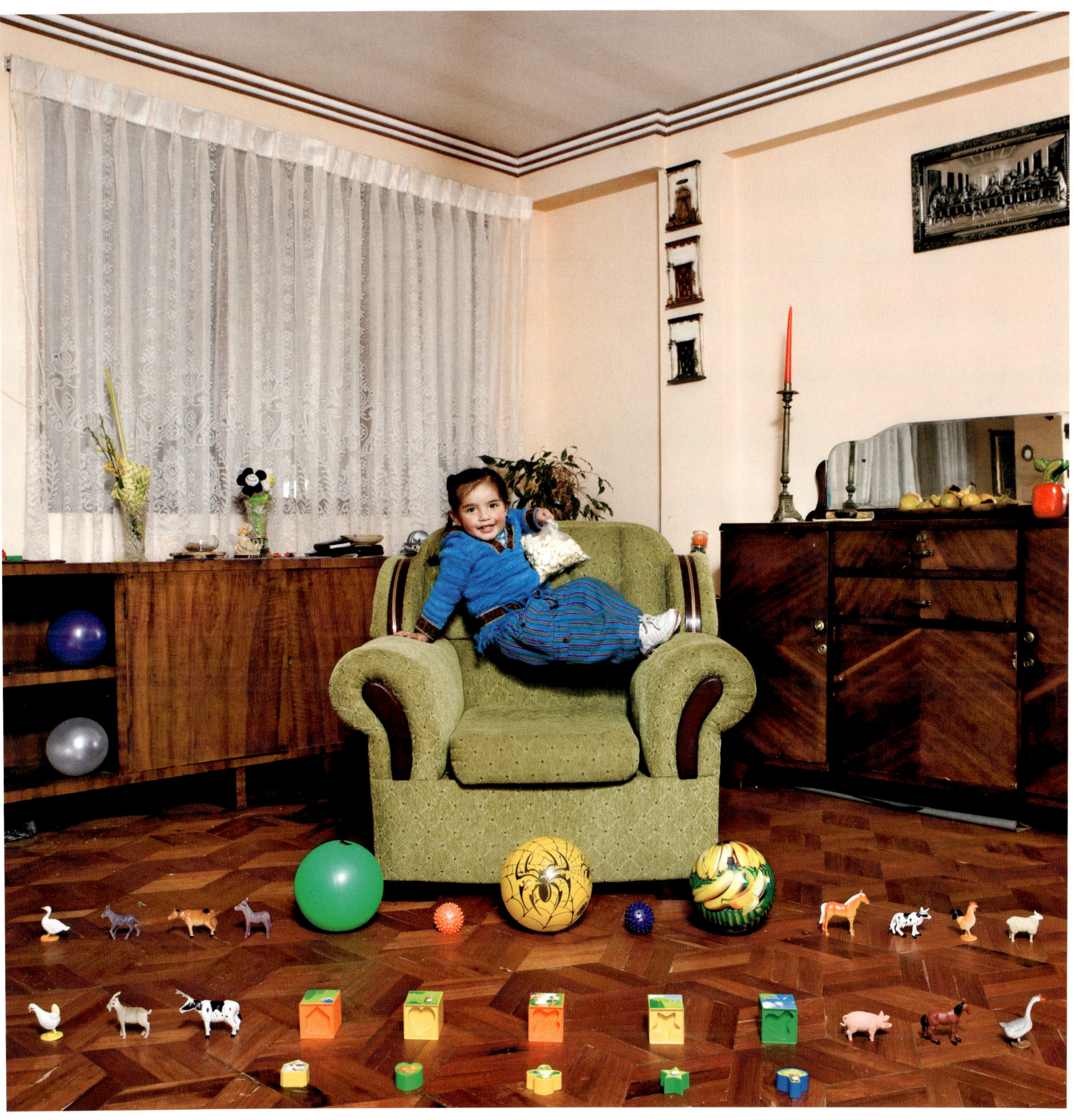

Keynor, 3

Cahuita, Costa Rica

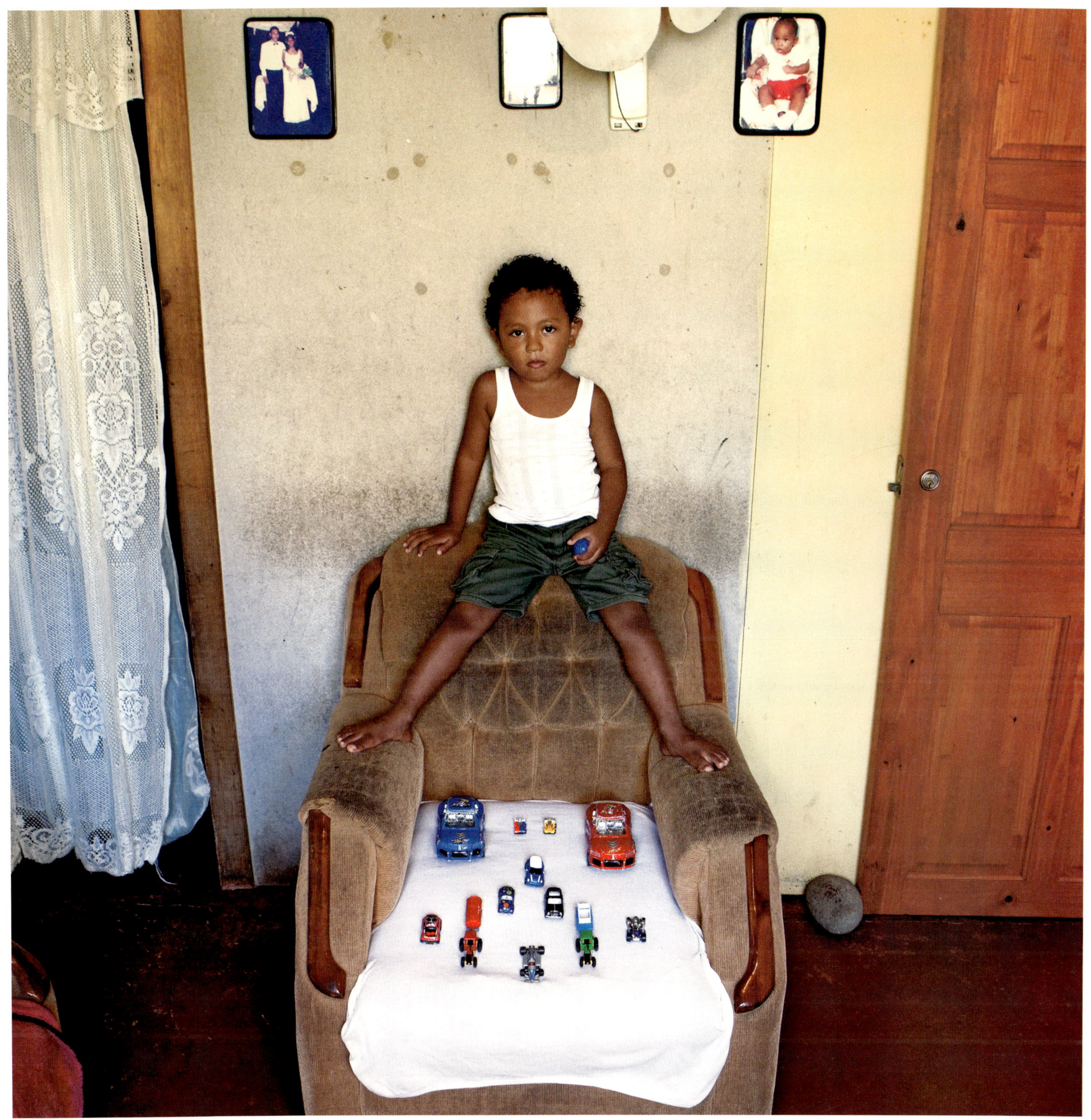

Shotaro, 5

Tokyo, Japan

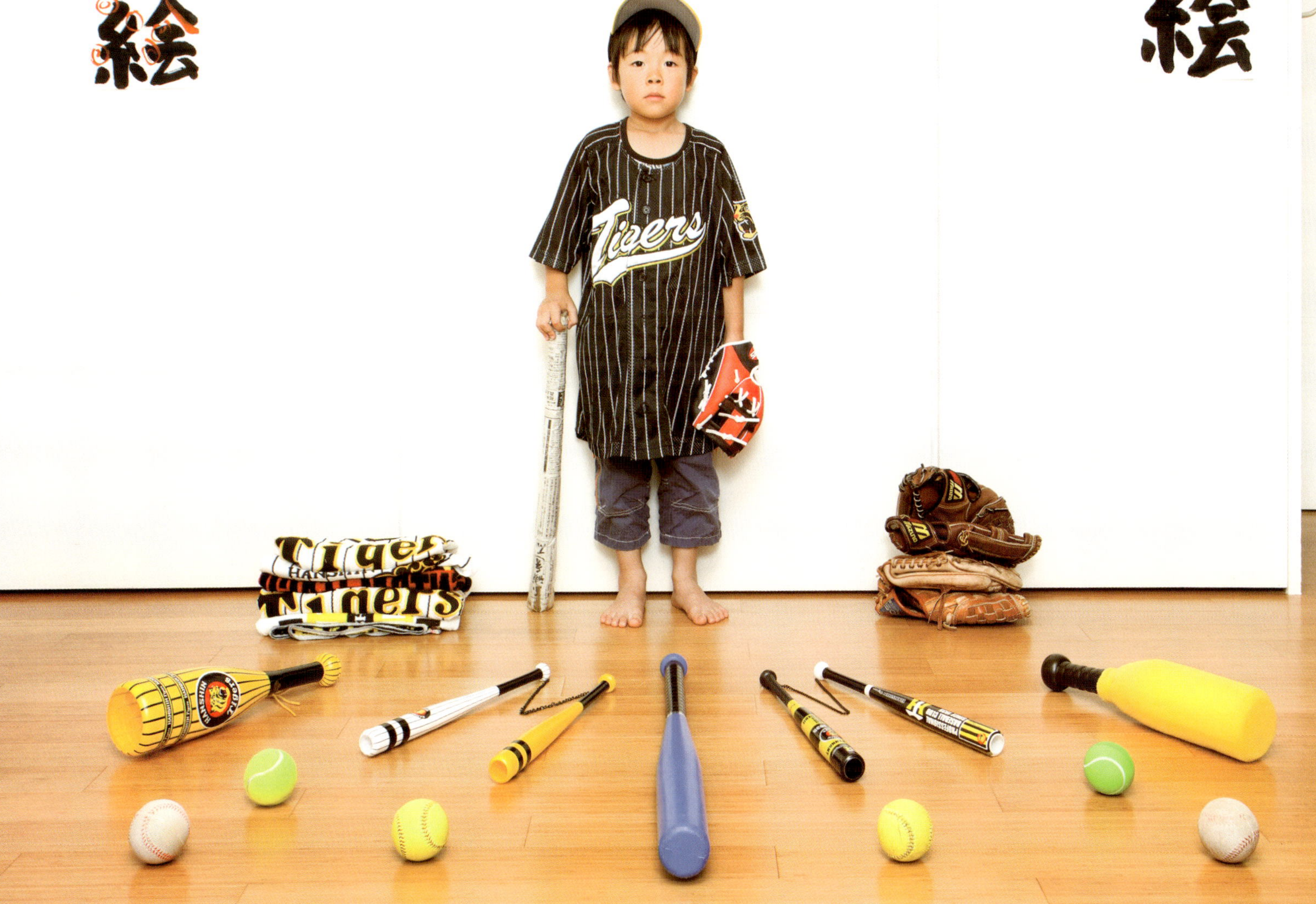
すみ絵
すみ絵
もえ
Tigers
Tigers
Tigers

Ernesto, 3

Florence, Italy

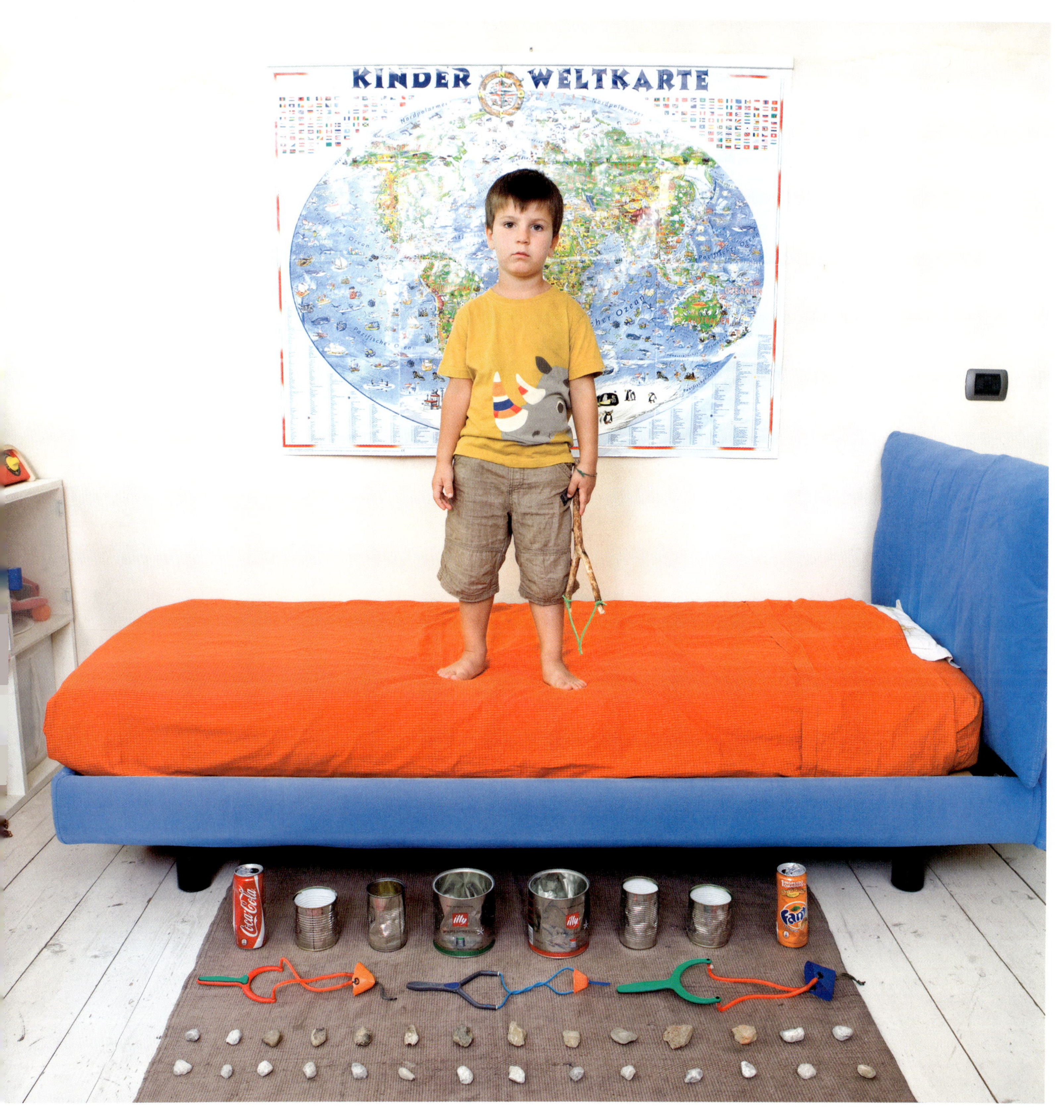
KINDER WELTKARTE
Coca-Cola
illy
illy
Fanta

Gabriele says thank you to:

My family, all the parents and families of the children photographed for this book, Arianna Rinaldo, Cristina Guarinelli, all the people of D di Repubblica, Paolo Woods, Edoardo Delille, Claude Baechtold, Serge Michel, Pietro Chelli, INSTITUTE, Stefano Stoll and all the friends of Riverboom, GP&Catiello and all my friends in Val di Chiana, Elisa Paolucci, Catalina Jurado, Alia Bengana, Vanessa Peters, Annina, the gang of Via Vigevano 9, all the people who hosted me and helped me during my long trip around the world, Studio Marangoni in Florence, Buckley Barratt, Nina and all the people at *Nido* magazine, couchsurfing.org, Carlo Landucci and occhidellasperanza.it.

I want to dedicate this book to my nephew Matteo a.k.a Jack.

Gabriele Galimberti is part of the art collective Riverboom (www.riverboom.com).

Editor: **David Cashion**
Designer: **Rachel Willey**
Production Manager: **Erin Vandeveer**

Library of Congress Control Number: 2013945686

ISBN: 978-1-4197-1174-9

Printed and bound in the United States
10 9 8 7 6 5 4 3 2 1

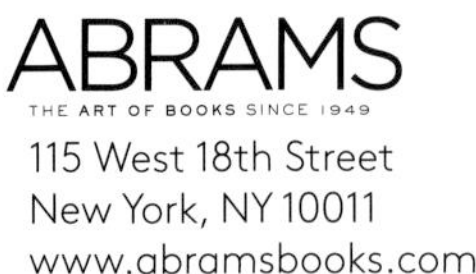

115 West 18th Street
New York, NY 10011
www.abramsbooks.com